Comments on other *Amazing Stories* from readers & reviewers

"*Tightly written volumes filled with lots of wit and humour about famous and infamous Canadians.*"
Eric Shackleton, *The Globe and Mail*

"*The heightened sense of drama and intrigue, combined with a good dose of human interest is what sets* Amazing Stories *apart.*"
Pamela Klaffke, *Calgary Herald*

"*This is popular history as it should be... For this price, buy two and give one to a friend.*"
Terry Cook, a reader from Ottawa, on **Rebel Women**

"*Glasner creates the moment of the explosion itself in graphic detail...she builds detail upon gruesome detail to create a convincingly authentic picture.*"
Peggy McKinnon, *The Sunday Herald,* on **The Halifax Explosion**

"*It was wonderful...I found I could not put it down. I was sorry when it was completed.*"
Dorothy F. from Manitoba on **Marie-Anne Lagimodière**

"*Stories are rich in description, and bristle with a clever, stylish realness.*"
Mark Weber, *Central Alberta Advisor,* on **Ghost Town Stories II**

"*A compelling read. Bertin...has selected only the most intriguing tales, which she narrates with a wealth of detail.*"
Joyce Glasner, *New Brunswick Reader,* on **Strange Events**

"*The resulting book is one readers will want to share with all the women in their lives.*"
Lynn Martel, *Rocky Mountain Outlook,* on **Women Explorers**

GREAT GOALTENDERS

GREAT GOALTENDERS

Stars of Hockey's Golden Age

HOCKEY

by Jim Barber

PUBLISHED BY ALTITUDE PUBLISHING CANADA LTD.
1500 Railway Avenue, Canmore, Alberta T1W 1P6
www.altitudepublishing.com
www.amazingstories.ca
1-800-957-6888

Publisher	Stephen Hutchings
Associate Publisher	Kara Turner
Editor	Frances Purslow and Ros Penty
Cover and Layout	Bryan Pezzi

We acknowledge the financial support of the Government
of Canada through the Book Publishing Industry Development
Program (BPIDP) for our publishing activities.

Altitude GreenTree Program 🌲
Altitude Publishing will plant twice as many trees as were used
in the manufacturing of this product.

Library and Archives Canada Cataloguing in Publication

Barber, Jim (Jim Christopher Matthew)
Great goaltenders / Jim Barber.

Includes bibliographical references.
ISBN 1-55439-084-2

1. Hockey goalkeepers--Biography. 2. Hockey players--Biography.
3. National Hockey League--Biography. I. Title.

GV848.5.A1B268 2006   796.962'092'2   C2005-906718-7

Printed and bound in Canada by Friesens
2 4 6 8 9 7 5 3 1

To the men in the iron and mesh cage, who risked life and limb, bare-faced, for the love of the game. And to the fans who loved to watch them.

Contents

Prologue

The war-weary fans who crammed into the arena in Halifax had seen a lot since the fall of 1939. For nearly five years, the city witnessed tens of thousands of Canadian soldiers, seamen, and flyers leave port to risk life and limb in battles in the Atlantic Ocean, the fields of France, the deserts of North Africa, and the skies over London.

But they hadn't seen the likes of Chuck Rayner before. Playing for an air force team, the netminder was tall, almost lanky. He had the reputation of thrilling fans with his propensity to wander from his crease to play the puck. Sometimes he barely got there before an onrushing forward swept it up.

On this night, the action was particularly hot and heavy, with great scoring chances at both ends of the ice. Rayner had made save after spectacular save. With teams comprising mainly solid amateur players, the quality of the hockey was decent, but a little ragged compared with the tempered ferocity and flashy brilliance of the National Hockey League that Rayner was used to.

Late in the game, the puck caromed back into Rayner's end of the ice. He rushed out of his crease to deflect the shot into the corner. Practically every skater from both teams followed it into the corner. Sticks banged, and players hooted and hollered as the frozen rubber disc somehow managed to squirt free from the melee.

Rayner had moved away from the crowd, and found himself in possession of the puck — alone and unfettered.

Placing both his blocker and gloved hand on his heavy goal stick, the smooth-skating netminder began to glide down the ice. By the time the other players noticed what was happening, Rayner had crossed centre ice, and was showing no signs of stopping. Memories of playing keep-away on the frozen prairie ponds and sloughs of his youth came flooding back.

At first bewildered by what they were witnessing, fans in Halifax soon began to stand and cheer. However improbable, his daring feat caught the imagination of the crowd, which roared its approval. With the clamour of the fans ringing in his ears, Rayner burst into the other team's end. Without hesitation, he launched a deceptively hard, and surprisingly accurate shot on the befuddled netminder. The roar became deafening when the twine at the back of the net bulged.

Once the shock wore off, Rayner's teammates clustered around him, patting him on the backside, mussing his hair. Rayner simply skated back down the ice, and readied himself for the next play. In a time when newspaper headlines were dominated with tales of bloodshed and woe, Chuck Rayner's exploits on a hockey rink brought a little bit of fun back into everyone's life.

Prologue

Chuck Rayner had defied tradition, logic, and his coaches with his bold burst up the ice. It wasn't the first time that he amazed and astonished a crowd, and it wouldn't be the last.

Introduction

There's no definitive empirical research to confirm that hockey goaltenders are different from other elite-level athletes, physically or psychologically. But anecdotal evidence proves otherwise.

They willingly stand in front of dozens of hard, fast projectiles, throwing various and sundry body parts in front of these pucks with the sole purpose of stopping them. Goalies face the fury of the other team and block shots at all cost. They possess speed, agility, and above all — courage.

In the pre-expansion period of the NHL — what is often referred to as the Golden Age of the NHL or the Original Six Era — these men, for the most part, didn't wear facial protection. If their reflexes failed them, permanent disfigurement, loss of sight, loss of teeth, and loss of consciousness were likely outcomes.

Many of the goalies from this era of hockey wore little more than extra pieces of felt padding sewn into their jerseys, and a modified baseball catcher's chest protector. After a game, a goaltender could often measure his success or failure by the number of bruises and welts that adorned his body. If he had a lot, his night had been busy, and not many goals were scored against.

Introduction

Not only do goalies have to contend with the ever-present danger to life and limb, but they also have to contend with the knowledge that they are the last line of defence, in full view of thousands upon thousands of spectators. If a puck gets past them, it's generally seen as their fault. It's the only position in which the entire fortune of a game, a playoff series, or a Stanley Cup title can be decided by one false move, one stumble, or one bad decision by a single player — the goalie.

When a forward makes a mistake, one of his linemates can cover it up. Or a defenceman can help out. If a defenceman goofs, he relies on the goalie to save his bacon. Who can make up for a goalie's miscue? Nobody. A goalie's mistake means a goal. Goaltenders have to endure the looks of disappointment from their teammates, the taunting of the opposition, or the rage of hometown fans.

Goalies have to be able to put the injury, the mistake, and the temporary sense of shame behind them, and be ready to make a save on the very next face-off. And in the world of the NHL before expansion in 1967, even the best goalies in the business rarely made more than $20,000 a season.

Gump Worsley must have been right when he said, "Not all goalies are crazy, of course. Only about 90 percent of them."

Chapter 1
Clint Benedict: The Unheralded Innovator

Not much is known about Clint Benedict's early life, but theatrical training must have been in there somewhere. Unlike contemporaries such as Georges Vezina or George Hainsworth, Benedict is a bit of an enigma. He may be the most anonymous of the early Hall of Fame goaltenders, even though, by all accounts, he was as talented as any other padded denizen of the goal cage.

The numbers alone don't give hockey fans a true picture of the man. Anyone whose career altered the way a position is played, the way an entire game is played, deserves due reverence.

Clint Benedict was a clever man, an innovative man,

someone who was willing to test the boundaries of a very conservative sporting establishment. Although not one to deliberately seek publicity off the ice, when he entered the icy field of play, he did whatever he thought was best to protect himself and help his team win the game. His name should be ranked beside Jacques Plante or Glenn Hall, but radical ideas or radical personalities were rarely embraced in sports in the early years of the 20th century.

Back then, goaltenders were not allowed to roam from the area in front of the net. They were not allowed to play the puck and they had to remain standing throughout the game. No dropping. No flopping. Goalies made saves using their body, their legs, and their stick. The use of one of the gloved hands to catch or trap the puck, in the manner of baseball players, was rarely seen in Canadian rinks.

Clint Benedict grew up in that environment, but he chafed under what he saw as oppressive and unnecessary hindrances to his ability to do his job.

In 1909, when Benedict was just 15 years old, the coach/manager of the Stewartons, a team in the Ottawa City League, must have sensed his extraordinary ability, because he enlisted him to play goal. The city league would have been comparable to intermediate level hockey being played elsewhere in the province. Although talented teens played here and there at this level, the vast majority of the players were grown men.

The fact that Benedict had been recruited to play at

this level bears witness to his poise and a maturity beyond his years. Being in a dressing room full of hardened hockey men would have been a daunting proposition for someone with less self-assurance. Facing shots from those same men in practice, as well as those from enemy shooters in games, also showed that Benedict was confident in himself as a man and as a goaltender.

The confidence, talent, and a relentless desire to bend the rules of the game to improve his lot as a goaltender are hallmarks of his illustrious career, which began in the nation's capital, not long after hockey became Canada's new national passion.

Along with Montreal, Ottawa was one of the early hotbeds of hockey. Like many of his chums growing up, Clint Benedict played the sport on any patch of ice available in winter.

He was born in the autumn of 1894, a year after the Montreal Amateur Athletic Association (AAA) defeated the Generals — a team from Ottawa — to win the Amateur Hockey Association (AHA) title, and be the first team memorialized on the newly minted Stanley Cup. The Ottawa side managed to wrest the Cup from Montreal the following year, delighting Lord Stanley of Preston back in England, the former governor-general of Canada, who purchased the large silver chalice that would bear his name.

While he served Queen Victoria as her representative to the Dominion of Canada, Stanley was an avid sportsman, like most members of the British aristocracy. While he enjoyed traditional British sports, he became smitten with this icebound game known as hockey.

Through his encouragement and patronage, the sport began to grow and flourish in Ottawa. By the time Benedict was born, it was a major winter sport, both in terms of participation and entertainment.

By the turn of the 20th century, the city of Ottawa boasted an extensive hockey system that included a city-wide league — the one Clint Benedict joined in 1909.

The following season, Benedict moved to the Ottawa New Edinburgh's team, where he remained for two seasons. That 1910–1911 season also marked the professional debut of one of Benedict's chief rivals, the man whose untimely death would add to his legend: Georges Vezina, of the Montreal Canadiens.

While Vezina was gaining a reputation on a national scale for his exploits for Le Club de Hockey Canadien, Benedict's esteem grew in his home city. He was regaled in the press for his spectacular, and somewhat unorthodox, style.

In 1910–1911, Benedict went 7-3-1 and 3-0 in the playoffs to help the New Edinburgh's to the league title. While high by today's standards, his 3.60 goals-against average (GAA) was considered to be miserly at that time.

The following year, he dominated the league, winning all 11 of his games with a 3.11 GAA, and again sparking his team to a championship. At the ripe old age of 18, Benedict was now regarded not only as a talented goaltender, but also as a winner. Benedict had that rare temperament that made him a winner. He would rise to the occasion when the chips were down, when the season was on the line, when the championship was within reach.

Benedict was a star on the rise, and with his success in the local league, it was only a matter of time before the professional ranks beckoned.

The manager of the Ottawa Senators signed Benedict to a professional contract in 1912. The Senators were created out of the ashes of the Generals. Although they wore red-, black-, and white-striped uniforms, they were dubbed "The Silver Seven" by fans and the media because legend had it that the team paid its players in silver nuggets. The team also won a lot of silver trophies, which may have added to the nickname's appeal.

Benedict was brought in to be the understudy of Ottawa's legendary goalie, Percy LeSueur. It must have been difficult for Benedict to spend most of his time riding the pine during his first two seasons as a professional. But there is no indication that he complained.

Benedict knew he had to pay his dues and make the most of his opportunities. Although the team finished with a disappointing record of 9-11 in 1912–1913, Benedict was given credit for seven of the wins, even though he only saw action in half of the team's games.

The following season, he went 5-3 in nine games. The Senators knew they had their goaltender of the future.

LeSueur, who could see the writing on the wall, left the team voluntarily before the start of the 1914–1915 campaign. He was dealt to the Toronto Ontarios, and soon left the players' ranks to move into coaching.

At age 20, Clint Benedict was now the number one goaltender in the second-most pressure-packed hockey market in the world.

Benedict amazed teammates and opponents alike, as he brilliantly filled the skates of the popular LeSueur. Playing in all 20 games, he won 14 and lost 6, helping the Senators place first in the National Hockey Association (NHA), with a chance to win the Stanley Cup against the Vancouver Millionaires of the Pacific Coast Hockey Association (PCHA).

The PCHA had been formed three years earlier by brothers Frank and Lester Patrick. Hockey stars in their own right in the formative years of the game, the Patricks used the proceeds from their father's lumber empire to create a new league on the western edge of the continent. They started with three teams in British Columbia: the Vancouver Millionaires, the Victoria Aristocrats, and the New Westminster Royals.

The PCHA pilfered some of the best players from the NHA, and soon lobbied the trustees of the Stanley Cup to give them equal standing with their eastern rivals. The rules were changed so the Cup would now only be contested between the winners of the NHA and PCHA.

Perhaps overconfident, the Senators failed to recognize that the Millionaires were more than able opponents, boasting no fewer than seven future Hall of Famers, led by Fred "Cyclone" Taylor. Even the brilliance of Benedict was no match for the western powerhouse, as Vancouver romped to 6-2, 8-3, and 12-3 victories over Ottawa, to bring the Stanley Cup out west for the first time.

"We were beaten so badly that we took the $147 share from the series and went to the World's Fair in San Francisco until the heat wore off. I seldom talk about that team. Usually, I cite the main reasons why we lost; their names were Frank Nighbor, Frank Patrick, and Cyclone Taylor," Benedict said years later.

It was at this time — once Benedict became a starter and a recognized star — that keen observers began to take note of his unique style.

Benedict was one of the first goaltenders to see the great benefit in using his hands as a defensive weapon. He caught the puck more than his contemporaries. He used his stick hand to intentionally deflect or block waist-high shots into the corner or away from the front of the goal. Since goalies at that time did not wear the padded blockers and trappers of today, Benedict's hands took a perpetual beating. Benedict was often forced to play hurt, as did all goalies of that era.

The pressure to perform, and the pressure to keep one's job meant that Benedict and his ilk would play through as much pain as they could, to avoid missing game action, and the possibility of being upstaged by a younger, hungrier (and usually cheaper) rival. Not only did Benedict routinely display his toughness, but he also displayed his creativity and penchant for self-preservation through innovation.

Whether Benedict picked up his unique style from watching comedic stage shows or early motion pictures is not known, but somewhere in his youth he learned how to fall down, and make it look real.

Benedict slowly began testing the limits of the NHA rule that maintained that all goaltenders had to remain standing or incur a penalty. Sometimes, he would pretend to slip and drop down to one knee at precisely the moment he needed to make a save. At other times, Benedict would lose his balance and end up on his side or back at an opportune moment.

He also began to skate out of his crease more to challenge shooters. Somehow, Benedict rarely had penalties called against him, even though he was obviously breaking the rules. He seemed to be able to smooth-talk referees.

Ottawa fans loved their goaltender with his unique style, although in opposing rinks, his pratfalls were often sources of derision and frustration. Fans in Toronto began calling him "Praying Bennie," because he was always dropping to his knees. Legend has it that he would tell referees that he was simply offering a prayer of thanksgiving — and do it with an angelic look on his face.

Modern goaltenders, such as Curtis Joseph and Dominik Hasek, can thank a smart young man from Ottawa for pioneering a style of goaltending that transformed the way hockey was played.

On the ice, besides the innovations and creativity Benedict was bringing to the game, the Senators, after a lacklustre first year in the NHL, bounced back by 1919–1920 to win the league title. Benedict was practically impenetrable against a very potent Seattle offence. His performance was key to Ottawa winning its first Stanley Cup as a member of the National Hockey League. It would not be its last.

The Senators and Benedict continued their roll into the 1920–1921 season. For the second consecutive year, Benedict was lauded as the best netminder in the NHL, even though the Senators had dropped to second place in league standings.

By now, Benedict was a wily veteran, and very much respected throughout the league. He certainly impressed a young rookie who joined the Senators before the 1921–1922 season — Francis "King" Clancy.

"He was superb. A lot of people say that Georges Vezina was the greatest goaltender in those early days of hockey, but if you look up the records, you'll see that Clint Benedict ... had a better average," Clancy said in his memoirs.

The road to the Stanley Cup would be a little tougher in 1922–1923, as a second professional league had been formed in Western Canada — the Western Canadian Hockey League. The winner of the series between the NHL and the Pacific Coast League (PCL) would then face the Edmonton Eskimos, champions of the new league, for the Stanley Cup.

Clint Benedict: The Unheralded Innovator

Ottawa clinched the best-of-five series against the Vancouver Millionaires and then went on to face Edmonton. Although the Eskimos were built up in the media as being superior opponents to Vancouver, Ottawa had little difficulty in sweeping them aside.

The 1923 Cup win would not be the last for the franchise, but it would be the last time they'd win with Clint Benedict as their goaltender.

The following season, it appeared that Benedict was beginning to have trouble handling longer shots. Was his eyesight fading? Against the powerhouse Montreal Canadiens in the NHA finals, facing the likes of Aurel Joliat, Howie Morenz, and Habs netminder Georges Vezina, Benedict wilted. Ottawa management saw cracks in their championship foundation and concluded that a changing of the guard was needed.

They decided that some of the veteran core that had helped them win three Stanley Cups in four years was now expendable. Ottawa was in desperate financial straits, which forced them to part with high-priced veterans such as Benedict. Clint Benedict, the only goaltender the team had known since the Senators joined the National Hockey League, was dealt (with Harry "Punch" Broadbent) to the expansion Montreal Maroons for cash. The replacements for these players proved to be almost as good and a good deal cheaper. As disappointed as Ottawa fans were, Benedict's replacement, Alex Connell, another homegrown product, soon won them over by breaking Benedict's shutout record with seven.

The Maroons were owned by a group of wealthy English-Canadian Montreal businessmen. They also arranged for the financing and construction of the most magnificent ice palace the world had ever seen up to that time — the Forum.

In the Maroons' first campaign, they struggled to find themselves, finishing near the bottom of the league. The team had little offence to speak of, and their record might have been much worse than 9-19-2, if not for Benedict's two shutouts and 2.11 GAA. The eyesight problems still plagued him at times, but he won over the Montreal crowd with his talent and tenacity.

By the following year, with the roster of veteran players finally gelling in front of Benedict, the Maroons were the class of the NHL, winning 20 and losing only 11 in the 36-game schedule.

Ottawa still had a better regular season, but in the playoffs, the veteran savvy of Benedict, and teammates Broadbent, Reg Noble, Nels "Old Poison" Stewart, and Babe Siebert eventually carried the day for the Maroons.

The Senators had a slight edge in the regular-season series, winning twice, losing only once, and tying the Maroons three times. But it was the Maroons who drew first blood in the first game of the league finals, on a soft goal by Broadbent that eluded Connell.

Then Benedict's poor eyesight came to the fore, as a long shot off the stick of Ottawa's Clancy handcuffed the veteran goalie late in the game.

This was a total-goals series, so the winner of the second game would earn the right to play for the Stanley Cup.

The discipline and experience of the Maroons was the deciding factor in the game. Benedict was sharp, stopping everything he saw. His defence made sure there were few long shots on goal, and clamped down on any Ottawa scoring forays. Benedict truly earned the shutout, and he and the Maroons were on their way out west to face the Victoria Cougars.

Concerns about his eyesight were allayed in the opening game of the finals, as Benedict stymied the Cougars for a 3-0 shutout victory. He was just as dominating in the second contest, which ended with the same score.

The Victoria Cougars, prodded by their manager Lester Patrick, managed to eke out a 3-2 win to stave off elimination, but Benedict picked up his third shutout in four games, as the Maroons won the game 2-0 and the series 3-1.

That would be the last time two leagues would compete for the Stanley Cup. The Patricks folded their western league, selling one of the teams — Victoria — to interests in Detroit, while the Portland team would become the Chicago Blackhawks. With the advent of the Boston Bruins and New York Rangers, the NHL comprised 10 teams, and the winner of the league would automatically be awarded the Stanley Cup.

Although they finished at only 0.500 (20 wins, 20 losses, and 4 ties in the now 44-game season), the Maroons still made the playoffs and faced the Canadiens in a two-game total goals series.

The teams tied 1-1 in the opener, with Benedict playing brilliantly for the underdog Maroons.

In the second game, even though some of the best goal scorers in the game were on the ice, the teams remained deadlocked at 0-0 heading into overtime. In the third extra frame, Canadiens star Howie Morenz fired a shot right from the face-off, which blew past Benedict, dethroning the champs. The Ottawa Senators would ultimately win the Stanley Cup that year. It was their last.

In 1928, Benedict led the Maroons back to the Cup finals against the New York Rangers. Like the Montrealers, the expansion Rangers were built with veteran talent, and proved their mettle by winning the Cup in the maximum five games.

By this point, Benedict's worsening eyesight was becoming more of a liability. He was still one of the best goaltenders in the game, but it was obvious that his skills were diminishing.

In the second game of the 1928 finals, Benedict gave up a long soft goal in overtime. Showing the resiliency and mental toughness that had been hallmarks of his days as a teenager back in Ottawa, he bounced back to register a shut-out in game three, but then lost the next two games, giving the Broadway Blueshirts and New York City their first ever Stanley Cup.

After an abysmal 1928–1929 season for Benedict personally and the Maroons as a team, both bounced back with a quick start to the 1929–1930 season.

Clint Benedict: The Unheralded Innovator

It was during this campaign at the twilight of his playing career that Benedict's innovative spirit came to the fore once again.

In a Maroons–Canadiens game in January 1930, Howie Morenz fired a high shot directly at Benedict. Partially screened by his defenceman, and with his eyesight growing dimmer, the Maroons netminder totally misread the trajectory of the puck. It nailed him on the nose and cheek. One observer claimed that Benedict's nose looked like a broken eggshell, as he was carried off the ice by players from both teams.

It was part of an already luckless season for the veteran goalie. A few nights earlier, he was hit by a less serious shot on the head. And before that, he had missed some games because of a bout of food poisoning.

Six weeks after the Morenz blast, Benedict retook his position in goal for the Maroons. A murmur rippled through the crowd. He was wearing a self-fashioned mask that covered a good portion of his face.

Clint Benedict had done it again. Not only did he revolutionize the way that goalies played their position, now he was reforming what they wore.

The ugly leather device was wholly impractical, as it prevented him from seeing shots at his feet and did little to deaden the impact of shots hitting his face. However, he wore the contraption for five games, winning two, losing two, and tying one — allowing 16 goals in all. His season came to an end when an errant elbow from Howie Morenz nailed Benedict in the throat during the fifth game.

"I was in bed for a month and eventually it was that injury that forced me out of hockey because my vision was affected," Benedict said shortly before his death in 1976.

It was the last time Benedict strapped on the pads in the National Hockey League. The mask never caught on in hockey circles, although it generated a lot of talk.

When Jacques Plante first donned his mask in the late 1950s, it took little time for it to spread throughout the league. Few hockey fans knew that another goaltender had already pioneered the concept more than 25 years earlier.

Chapter 2
Chuck Rayner:
Broadway's Best

rowing up on the wide-open prairies of Saskatchewan, Claude Earl Rayner loved hockey.

Born in 1920, he followed the sport as a youngster, usually over the radio or through the newspapers. Although he was Canadian, Rayner held a soft spot in his heart for the New York Americans.

"I used to follow the National League as a kid, right up until I turned pro. I was a great hockey fan, and I admired the way a lot of those people played. Of course, the Americans were always at the bottom of the league, and the funny thing is — they were one of my favourite teams. They didn't win very much. I don't know why I liked them; I guess I always felt sorry for them."

The Americans had joined the National Hockey League

in 1925, just a year after the Boston Bruins. Unlike the team from Beantown, the Americans never managed to cobble together much in the way of on- or off-ice success. In other words, they never won any championships, and could never seem to get their financial house in order.

The Bruins won the Stanley Cup in their fourth season and are still considered one of the cornerstone franchises of the league, while the Americans often struggled just to make the playoffs and eventually faded into obscurity.

They did make the playoffs once in their first 10 seasons, and that was in 1929. That year they finished second in the Canadian division, mostly thanks to the incredible performance between the pipes of Roy Worters, their goaltender. Worters' play was so phenomenal, he was awarded the Hart Trophy as the NHL's most valuable player — the first goalie to earn such an accolade. Nine-year-old Rayner cheered the pint-sized goalie every step of the way, never dreaming that he would one day duplicate Worters' feat.

Although they were the first team from the Big Apple to play in the NHL, the Americans would see their star eclipsed by a second New York team, which also played out of Madison Square Garden — the New York Rangers.

The Rangers had better management from the get go, with their first team assembled by future Toronto Maple Leafs owner/manager/coach, Conn Smythe. Later, Smythe was replaced by the future Hall of Fame player/builder/manager/coach, Lester Patrick.

The Americans could never seem to ice a solid lineup. But their management team did one thing right: in 1939 they signed Rayner, now going by the moniker Chuck, to a minor pro contract. The lanky goaltender was the only ray of sunshine on the horizon for the Americans. They entered the 1940s with a depleted roster because of the war, and a depleted bank balance because of less than stellar attendance, and an ownership group that was always in financial difficulty. Rayner played his first 12 NHL games for the Americans at the end of the 1940–1941 season, and although he only won two and tied three, he was generally credited for giving the team a modicum of respectability.

After playing only one game the following year for the Springfield Indians of the American Hockey League, where he played the bulk of the previous season as well, he was up with the now renamed Brooklyn Americans for most of the 1941–1942 campaign.

By the time the Americans franchise folded before the start of the 1942–1943 season, Rayner was already in training for the Canadian Navy. "I had some friends go in the Navy, so I joined them. I was on the North Atlantic with the convoys. I was on there for three years, and it was great. It was dangerous … We were very fortunate. We were in with all the Wolf Packs — the U-boats. They were all around us, but never seemed to hit us."

When he wasn't on the high seas, Rayner still managed to strap on the pads frequently. Later in the war, he played for a touring team of top hockey-playing soldiers, many of whom were fellow NHLers like himself.

With the armed forces team in Halifax one night, Rayner was feeling a little frisky. His days on the frozen ponds in frigid Saskatchewan came flooding back.

The play had come in close to his crease, and practically every player from both teams was clogged up in, around, or behind Rayner's goal.

"I stopped a shot, and the puck bounced straight out," he said in an interview. "I skated out to get clear [of the melee around him], found myself alone, and went the rest of the way. When I got about 15 feet from the other goal, I shot and scored."

This marked the first time in the recorded history of hockey that a goaltender had scored a goal in that manner. There had been the odd one lobbed from one end of the ice to another, often into an empty net when the opposing goalie had been pulled for an extra attacker, but never had a goalie lumbered down the ice, stick handling the puck as best he could, and then scoring.

One has to wonder if the other netminder that night in Halifax didn't react to Rayner's shot because he was stunned by the unexpected foray. Rayner would attempt the trick once in a while thereafter, but never repeated his war-time feat.

Rayner had learned to skate, stickhandle, and roam around his own end during his days playing with the Saskatoon Wesleys and the Kenora Thistles.

But he also gave a great deal of credit to an unexpected source — Springfield Indians eccentric and tyrannical owner/manager/coach Eddie Shore — a man who once tied another goaltender to the net, so he wouldn't drop to the ice.

Shore made Rayner skate around the ice as much as his less-heavily clad teammates, building up his skating strength and stamina. He also made Rayner repeatedly shoot pucks against the boards to build up his wrist strength. Rayner played 38 games in total for Shore, from 1940 to 1942.

After being discharged from the navy when the war ended, Rayner was ready to take up hockey again. Because he had played a fair bit of hockey, especially in 1944 and 1945, he was still sharp. Because he had proved his mettle to the rest of the NHL by enduring the disaster with the Americans with confidence intact, the Rangers signed him before the start of the 1945–1946 season.

The next few years were a struggle for the Rangers, although Rayner acquitted himself well. The 1949–1950 campaign, however, would be the most glorious in his career, with the New York Rangers making it into the Stanley Cup finals for the first time in a decade. There they would face the powerhouse Detroit Red Wings.

After five games, the Rangers actually held the upper hand, leading the series three games to two. In the sixth game, in the third period, New York couldn't hold a slim 4-3 lead against the likes of Sid Abel, Ted Lindsay, and Gordie Howe.

Chuck Rayner

The Jack Adams–coached Detroit team battled back for a 5-4 win, sending the series to a seventh and deciding game.

Although the New York Rangers were the home team, they would not be playing the deciding game in Madison Square Garden. For many years, the Rangers were exiled from their own building when the circus came to town. They might have been a professional sports team whose stars were the toasts of Broadway, but the New York Rangers played second fiddle to the circus, which drew a larger crowd. The Rangers were playing the crucial game to appreciative Toronto fans at Maple Leaf Gardens. The tension in the building was palpable on that fine, spring evening.

Early in the game, New York burst out to a 2-0 lead and were still leading 3-2 late in the contest. Then the wily Wings managed to score the tying goal. The stage was set for one of the most dramatic moments in team sports — sudden death overtime in the seventh and championship-deciding game for the Stanley Cup.

The crowd at Maple Leaf Gardens was mesmerized. Programs were gripped tightly in nervous hands, stogies protruded between clenched teeth, and beads of perspiration formed on furrowed brows. The Maple Leaf crowd favoured the Rangers, because they despised the Detroit Red Wings. And the Rangers were undeniably the underdog in this match.

Rayner staged a remarkable performance, standing on his head to make saves. Then his teammate Nick Mickoski bore down with the puck on the Red Wings netminder. He had the goalie beat, but not his pal, Mr. Goalpost. With a dull clang, the Rangers' celebration plans were put on ice.

Not long thereafter, a face-off was called deep in the Rangers' zone. Rayner had been in a zone all season, and all playoffs long. Fans and sportswriters were already saying that he might be the first goalie since 1929 to be named the league's most valuable player.

It would take a play of absolute brilliance, or fool's luck to beat Rayner on this night. But, as often happens in sports lore, some previously unheralded player etches his name in the record books in a most unlikely fashion. In the second overtime period, George Gee won the draw back to Pete Babando. Seeing a clog of legs, arms, and bodies in front of Rayner, Babando lobbed the puck towards the New York goal, and the light went on behind Rayner. With that ugly goal, the dream season was over for Rayner and the Rangers.

"Not a day goes by that I don't think about that goal," Rayner said on many occasions in the years before his death. "What a shame that was. Just one goal, and there never would have been a 54-year drought." Rayner was referring to the fact that the Rangers had to wait until 1994 before they could bring the Stanley Cup back to New York.

The consolation prize came for Rayner at the end of the season, when he won the Hart Trophy as the league's most valuable player. It was a feat that put him in rare company. Only his boyhood idol, Roy Worters, had won the top individual honour for an NHL player while tending goal.

Even up to his death in 2002, Rayner credited his teammates as much as his own play for the award. "I could have never done it alone. We had some great hockey players that worked like hell for us and I think that's why I got the trophy.

But certainly to this day, I share it with the group of people that I played with."

Looking at his NHL statistics alone, it's hard to believe that Rayner ever made it to the Hockey Hall of Fame. But he was inducted in 1973, proving you don't need a bunch of championship trophies on your mantle to be a great player.

The numbers alone don't tell the complete tale. With very little scoring in front of him, and a lacklustre defence backing him up, Rayner was left to his own devices, and probably had more pucks fly at him than any other goaltender of his era. Who can say whether a Bill Durnan or Turk Broda — two of Rayner's contemporaries — would have been able to handle the constant losing, the poor play in front of him, and the overall sense of defeat that seemed to hang around the collective necks of the Rangers like an albatross? Rayner's successor between the pipes for the Rangers was Lorne "Gump" Worsley. When asked which NHL team gave him the most trouble, Worsley replied, "the Rangers."

Mental toughness, a pure enjoyment of the game, and the same spirit that led him to cheer for the underdog New York Americans back when he was a kid kept him playing his best and relishing the opportunity to play a kid's game for a living. These qualities plus his obvious talent propelled Claude Earl Rayner into the Hall of Fame.

Rayner, one of the thousands of Rangers fans who had endured five decades of frustration and futility, rejoiced when captain Mark Messier hoisted the Stanley Cup over his head in 1994. When The Moose did that act, many who had worn the uniform before him helped him lift it in spirit.

"I was very happy in 1994. I'm a Rangers fan and New York treated me very well. I have no complaints at all," he said just months before his death. "I would have liked to have been on better hockey clubs, of course. Naturally, you always do … We had the nucleus of a good hockey club, but nothing great."

Many Rangers fans of the 1940s and early 1950s would dispute that last sentence. There was certainly something great about "Bonnie Prince Charlie" Rayner.

Chapter 3
Terry Sawchuk:
Tortured Brilliance

erry Sawchuk grew up in a tough, working-class, ethnically diverse neighbourhood in Winnipeg, Manitoba. Tragedy struck the Sawchuk family not long after Terry was born on December 28, 1929. Before he was old enough to walk, his older brother Roger died of scarlet fever, and the family not only had to endure the pain of the youngster's death, but also the anguish and deprivation brought on by the Great Depression.

Terry idolized his another older brother, Mitch, who was a pretty good goaltender on the outdoor rinks in and around their neighbourhood. Mitch Sawchuk doted on his little brother, who was seven years his junior, and didn't mind too much when little Terry tagged along.

So, it was an emotionally crippling blow when Mitch

died of a sudden heart attack when he was 17, and Terry was only 10.

His parents became emotionally distant after losing another child, and Terry learned that the best way to go through life was to keep his feelings bottled up inside. This led him, in later life, to become an alcoholic, and someone prone to fits of both anger and melancholy.

All of young Terry's energies were channelled into hockey. One of his biographies described how he eschewed many of the normal pastimes and activities of other kids his age because he was so focused on becoming a professional hockey player, like his idol, George Hainsworth, who played for the Montreal Canadiens and Toronto Maple Leafs in the 1920s and 1930s.

Sawchuk loved hockey, but he also had a passion for baseball and football in the summer. One Sunday, when he was supposed to be off to Mass, he decided to heed the call from some of his chums and dashed over to a field to play a little pick-up ball — wearing his Sunday best. On one play, he fell awkwardly and broke his arm. Not wanting to get into trouble from his mother, he never told her how badly injured he was. She found out when he went to the doctor two years later about another injury. The bone had not set properly, causing his right arm to be two inches shorter than his left.

But the setbacks only steeled Sawchuk's resolve. He vowed that he was going to succeed, and would work as hard as he could to make his dream come true.

Terry Sawchuk: Tortured Brilliance

At the tender age of 12, the young goalie caught the attention of a local midget hockey coach, who was also a scout for the Detroit Red Wings. He helped refine Sawchuk's skills, which included the development of his unique style — the crouch. This stance, which is so familiar to modern-day hockey fans, was unusual in Sawchuk's day. It allowed him to maintain his balance in a number of positions, as well as make his lateral movement quicker.

Two years later, at age 14, Sawchuk had a chance to work out with the Red Wings, impressing the coaches and management team. He was not yet the property of the Detroit team, and had spurned an offer to sign with the Chicago Blackhawks in early 1946. His father, Louis, felt that the Wings were a more solid organization, with better prospects than the perennially woeful Windy City squad.

Later that year, Terry Sawchuk signed a C Form with the Red Wings, and played for their junior team in Galt, Ontario. The following season, the Galt team moved to Windsor to become the Spitfires, but Sawchuk only played a handful of games before moving up to the pro ranks with the Omaha Knights of the U.S. Hockey League.

In 54 games as a 17 and 18 year old, Sawchuk won 30, lost 18, and tied 5. He also chalked up four shutouts, and easily won rookie-of-the-year honours for the league in the 1947–1948 season.

The rapid ascent to the top was nearly derailed in the middle of his great rookie pro season. Hard luck seemed to hit Sawchuk at the most inopportune times. On the night of his 18th birthday, the Knights were playing Houston. Suddenly, there was a clutter of players and sticks in front of him. Spotting the loose puck amidst the tumult, Sawchuk dove towards it as he tried to smother it and stop the play.

But one of the Houston players jockeying for position lifted his stick, the blade gouging into Sawchuk's face. His eye took the brunt of the blow. Doctors warned that there was a good chance he would never regain the sight in his eye — a thought that must have tormented the young man to no end.

In a stroke of good fortune, however, his sight returned, and he was back on the ice within a couple of weeks. In a pattern that would be oft repeated throughout his career, Sawchuk returned with increased ferocity after the setback. In this instance, he posted a shutout in his first game back in a Knights' uniform.

He also won top rookie honours in the American Hockey League the following season, and was impressive in a seven-game audition for the Red Wings.

Detroit manager Jack Adams earned the nickname "Trader Jack" because he was always fussing and tinkering with the lineup, even though he had one of the best teams in the NHL. Adams believed that once a team tasted success, they would get soft and lackadaisical in their approach to the game, so fresh blood needed to be brought in. Adams thought incumbent goaltender Harry Lumley was getting complacent, and possibly out of shape. Lumley and four other Wings from the championship team were shipped to Chicago for four Hawks, and Terry Sawchuk, at age 20 was called up and became the starting goaltender for the defending Stanley Cup champions.

Fending off shots from the likes of Rocket Richard, Milt Schmidt, and Teeder Kennedy, Sawchuk played more like a mature veteran than a raw rookie. He played all 70 games on the schedule, winning 44, 11 of which were shutouts. He was named to the league's first All Star team, and also won the Calder Trophy as the NHL's rookie of the year.

Before the start of the next training camp, Adams ordered Sawchuk to go on a crash diet because he thought he was carrying around too much extra baggage. Adams was a fanatic about his players being in shape. Sawchuk loved food, and his weight was never an impediment to his performance. Food was something he enjoyed. It gave him comfort. When it was taken away from him, he became miserable. Many friends and long-time teammates point to the enforced food control as what brought out the cranky side of Sawchuk's personality. Not being able to enjoy food, he increased his drinking, and his behaviour changed. He was abrupt with reporters, distant to teammates, and downright rude, at times, to autograph-seekers.

On the ice, he was still the best in the game — a dichotomy not lost on his teammate, Ted Lindsay. "You could throw him a handful of rice and he'd catch every kernel. But he was also a miserable son of a bitch."

The following season, the Red Wings faced Toronto in the semi-finals, and won the opening game, 3-0. In the second game, the Maple Leafs pulled out all the stops. Veteran forward Teeder Kennedy had a couple of clear breakaways on the young netminder, but Sawchuk stoned him.

Max Bentley, one of the smoothest skaters and best stickhandlers in the NHL, tried his luck late in the game. He dipsy-doodled around a Detroit defenceman and came straight for Sawchuk. The goaltender knew that Bentley's linemate, Sid Smith, was also coming in on him, but was confident Bentley was going to make the play on him.

"I figured Max would try to deke me," he said later. "I made up my mind not to move. Bentley faked me, then passed across to Smith, who let a shot go. It was really labelled, but I managed to kick in time to stop it with my foot."

Many who saw it called it the most spectacular save they had ever seen. Not only did it solidify Sawchuk's reputation as a master of the nets, but it gave him his second straight shutout and a 2-0 series lead. After a lopsided win in the third game, Sawchuk came up with a game-saving save on Tod Sloan to help the Wings sweep the Leafs aside.

In the first game of the Stanley Cup finals against Montreal, Sawchuk would not surrender a goal until the middle of the third period, even though he was under ferocious assault from their forwards. The Wings won the game 3-1. He was also spectacular in the second game, which the Red Wings won 2-1. That goal would be the last Montreal would score against him in this series. The Wings would win the last two games of the playoffs by identical 3-0 scores. They were the third and fourth shutouts for Sawchuk in the post-season — a record. His GAA was an amazing 0.62. He also earned his first Vezina Trophy.

The 1952–1953 season would be a frustrating one for Sawchuk and the Red Wings. Both he and the team got off to a slow start. In a late October game, Sawchuk was beaten nine times in a 9-0 romp by Montreal.

Sawchuk's moodiness was now a cause for concern in the dressing room. He needed to be emotionally coddled by his teammates and coach Tommy Ivan. He was hypersensitive and would obsess about every goal he let in. In short, it was often a drag to be around him.

In late December, Alex Delvecchio blasted a shot in practice that hit an unprotected part of Sawchuk's foot. While he missed the next six games, his replacement, Glenn Hall, played very well in relief. Sawchuk soon began to worry that his fate would be the same as Lumley's — the man he made redundant only two seasons earlier.

Sawchuk finished the season and won the Vezina for the second straight year. In the semi-finals, an overconfident Detroit team lost four games to two to the underdog Boston Bruins. Many in the media blamed a sub-par performance by Sawchuk as the prime reason for the loss, and even Adams wondered if his formerly infallible netminder might be slipping.

The next year's training camp saw Sawchuk having to compete with Hall to see who would tend the Red Wings nets. Sawchuk won that battle, but for the remainder of his tenure in Detroit, he was always looking behind him, knowing that if he slipped, Adams would not hesitate to replace him with Hall.

The Red Wings won the Stanley Cup at the end of the 1953–1954 season, and repeated the feat the following season. Sawchuk won another Vezina at the end of that championship season, but changes were afoot. Adams decided the Red Wings needed another shake up.

In a couple of major deals, days apart in the early summer of 1955, a number of players were sent from the Wings. Boston Bruins manager, Lynn Patrick, said that when he and Adams were talking about dealing for a goaltender, Patrick had assumed Adams referred to the unproven but talented Glenn Hall. It was unthinkable that Adams would trade the best goaltender in the game. But he did.

"I think it was the darkest day of Terry's life," Sawchuk's wife, Pat, told author David Dupuis. "He cried and cried. I mean, the guys were all so close and then to have to hear about it on the radio ... It just ripped him apart. He gave everything for that organization and he felt like a piece of meat afterwards. All the trust he ever had in management or team spirit just went."

Although he put on a brave face in public, Sawchuk was never happy in Boston, and his performance reflected that. In 68 games in 1955–1956, he won only 22, lost 33, and tied 13. His GAA ballooned to 2.60. The following year, he quit the team after 34 games. He sat on the sidelines until he was dealt back to his beloved Wings in July 1957.

Although happy to be back in Detroit, the teams he backstopped were growing increasingly mediocre, and he was becoming more and more unhealthy. He continued to drink, and he was still moody.

It looked like the end of the road for Terry Sawchuk when he was left exposed in the intra-league draft in June 1964. But Toronto Maple Leafs coach/manager Punch Imlach had become an expert at reclamation projects.

Imlach's roster featured many veteran players who had been discarded by their former teams. His genius was that he knew the strengths and weaknesses of all his players, and knew how to motivate them to play to their maximum potential, without burning them out. Acquiring Sawchuk meant that he could lighten the load of goalie Johnny Bower, one of Imlach's first and best finds. With Bower and Sawchuk, he had the best one-two punch in goal in the league. This was borne out when both tenders shared the Vezina Trophy at the end of the 1964–1965 season.

Bower and Sawchuk were polar opposites in personality and work habits, but both were well liked and valued by their teammates. "Johnny would practice with you, whereas Sawchuk wouldn't practice," said Senator Frank Mahovlich in a 2004 interview. "But when it came game time, both were great. They were both just up for it. Terry would withdraw and be quiet, whereas Johnny would be out there kibitzing."

His sentiments were echoed by former Leaf and Red Wing star, Red Kelly. "Johnny and Terry did their jobs. You don't win unless you have good goaltending, and we had good goaltending. When one got hurt, the other one was there. And if one was having trouble, the other one stepped in and would come up big, so we were pretty fortunate to have both of them at the same time," he said.

The Leafs were not expected to do much in the 1966–1967 campaign — the last year of the six-team NHL. The "Over-the-Hill Gang" was a heavy underdog going up against the powerful Chicago Blackhawks in the semi-finals. The Hawks had Glenn Hall in goal, Stan Mikita and the Hull brothers — Dennis and Bobby — up front, as well as future Hall of Famer Pierre Pilote on the blue line. Toronto had a lineup of aging stars, two goaltenders with a combined age of over 80, and a few plucky youngsters, such as Ron Ellis.

The series was tied 2-2 heading into the fifth game. Bower had played the bulk of the series so far, but struggled in the opening period of game five. Sawchuk was sore, really sore, and was hoping for a rest. But when Imlach asked him if he could sub in for the struggling Bower, he simply nodded and prepared for the onslaught that awaited him.

One of the most famous incidents in Sawchuk's roller-coaster ride of a career took place in the first couple of min-

Goaltenders Terry Sawchuk and Johnny Bower
celebrate the Maple Leafs' 1967 Stanley Cup victory.

utes of the second period of that game. The teams were tied
2-2, and the crowd inside the Chicago Stadium was at their
raucous best.

Bobby Hull was deep inside the Toronto zone with the
puck, when he suddenly spun around and let one of his pat-
ented howitzers go. It was an impossible angle, and Sawchuk

51

was not prepared for the ferocity of the shot. It nailed Sawchuk's ailing shoulder, and the goaltender went down in a spasm of pain.

Toronto's trainer, Bob Haggert, came out to check on the fallen warrior. The late, great sportswriter Dick Beddoes got the story from Haggert's point of view.

"Where'd you get it, Ukey?" Haggart asked.

"On my bad shoulder," Sawchuk said, struggling to his knees.

"Think you're okay? Can you stay in the game?"

"I stopped the —ing shot, didn't I?" Sawchuk barked. "Help me get up and I'll stone those sons of bitches."

He stopped all 36 remaining shots he faced in that game. Both his teammates and his opponents lauded Sawchuk after one of the greatest displays of toughness and fortitude they had ever seen from a netminder.

After the game, the Golden Jet, Bobby Hull, said, "I saw him make those saves, but I still can't believe it. That was the most frustrating experience of my career. I've never seen such goaling."

Sawchuk was back in net as the Leafs won game six, and the series. In Canada's centennial year, the Maple Leafs were in the Stanley Cup finals and would face off against the Canadiens.

Taking advantage of Sawchuk's fatigue and injury, Montreal picked him apart in the series opener, winning 6-2. Bower came back for the second game and was superb, shutting out Henri Richard, Jean Beliveau, and the rest of the Habs 3-0. Bower also backstopped the Leafs' 3-2 win in the third game. It looked as though Bower was going to carry the load for the remainder of the series, a proposition that suited the banged up and exhausted Sawchuk just fine.

Then in the warm-up before the fourth game, Bower pulled a hamstring. Bower was done for the series, and Sawchuk would have to drag his aching, weary body back out and try to win the series.

His first game back wasn't pretty, as he surrendered six goals in a 6-2 loss. If Montreal was to win the fifth game on home ice, they would most likely take the series. Sawchuk needed to get back into top form, and he did, making a brilliant toe save on the first shift of the game. The Leafs went on to win 4-1, and Sawchuk was the star of the game.

The sixth game of the series would be the last kick at the championship can for many veteran Leafs. The NHL was expanding to 12 teams, and many of the players on the roster would be snapped up by the six new teams in the expansion draft, or they would retire.

Sawchuk blanked Jean Beliveau twice in the first period, leaving the graceful Montreal captain shaking his head in disbelief. Sawchuk stopped 17 shots in all from a very aggressive, but increasingly frustrated Canadiens forward contingent. The Leafs won 3-1 and Sawchuk had won his fourth, and possibly most satisfying Stanley Cup. After the game, he sounded like a man who was finished as a professional hockey player.

"I've had a lot of wonderful moments in hockey and other Stanley Cups, but nothing equal to this. It would be nice to go out a winner, the first star in a Cup-winning game. I have a wife, six kids, and another on the way. And I miss them very much during the hockey season. I'm not saying this was my last game, but I'm going to give it a lot of thought in the next few weeks."

He decided not to retire, and was chosen first in the expansion draft by the Los Angeles Kings.

Sawchuk should have gone with his gut and quit while he was ahead. Los Angeles was a debacle. He was miserable being so far from home, and his 3.42 GAA was the highest of his career.

The next couple of years saw him traded back to the Detroit Red Wings, followed by a tenure with the New York Rangers. Then, in the 1970 off-season, he got into a scuffle with Rangers teammate Ron Stewart, and died after suffering a pulmonary embolism.

He was 40 years old, and would be elected to the Hockey Hall of Fame the following year, after officials waived the normal three-year rule. Sawchuk had a troubled life, and was not always the most pleasant person to deal with, but his hockey statistics are memorable.

He won 446 games (second only to Patrick Roy), won four Vezina Trophies, and was voted to the first All-Star team three times. His 103 shutouts gave him nine more than his idol, George Hainsworth. His legacy as one of the best goaltenders in the game, maybe even *the* best, will be debated as long as there are hockey fans. One thing isn't debatable — Sawchuk was a unique personality, both on and off the ice.

Chapter 4
Jacques Plante:
Who Was That
Masked Man?

t the time, it seemed to be an innocent little tiff. But in hindsight, it came to define the personality and career of the individual many consider to be the finest goaltender to ever grace an ice surface in the National Hockey League.

And it was all over a toque — quintessential French-Canadian winter headwear.

It was the late fall of 1952, and Dick Irvin, the hard-nosed coach of the Montreal Canadiens, was in the midst of his 13th season behind the bench of the historic franchise, and his 23rd year of coaching in the NHL.

With that much experience, and a couple of Stanley Cups under his belt, he knew what sorts of players he wanted on his team. Irvin was old-school. He didn't tolerate players who didn't conform to what he perceived as proper conduct befitting a professional. He definitely didn't like quirky players — those with unique personalities.

Twenty-three-year-old goaltending phenom Jacques Plante did not just have a few minor idiosyncrasies — he was cut from a completely different cloth than most other hockey players of the time. Goaltenders in general have been described as being a breed apart from other position players. Plante was in a class by himself.

Since the 1949–1950 season, he had been doing a stellar job of netminding in the Montreal Canadiens minor league system, creating a name for himself as being one of the most spectacular and innovative goalies since Georges Vezina. He was a standout, mostly for the Montreal Royals of the Quebec Senior League, but also during a stint with the Buffalo Bisons of the American Hockey League (AHL).

Since his days in junior hockey, he was seen as the logical successor to Bill Durnan, the great Canadiens netminder of the 1940s, who won six Vezina Trophies over his seven-year NHL career. Gerry McNeil actually succeeded Durnan after the playoffs of 1950, and was a solid player, but Montreal's manager Frank Selke, and his assistant, Sam Pollock, knew Plante was destined to be their goaltender of the future, quirks and all.

When McNeil got injured in November 1952, Plante got the call.

In the minor leagues, he had earned the nickname "Jake the Snake" for his ability to slither around the ice, making save after spectacular save. He was also causing a stir for the then unheard of practice of venturing out of his goal crease to corral loose pucks. He often used the opportunity to not only forestall an opposing team's forecheck, but also to make an outlet pass to one of his defencemen.

But he was most affectionately known for his childlike habit of wearing a toque while playing. In a sense, it was a throwback to a different era, when goaltenders, and even some forwards and defencemen, wore toques or other warm headgear to stave off the frigid temperatures in the unheated rinks. In the early 1950s, Plante's toque created a buzz throughout the league, almost as much as his phenomenal play, and unique, rule-bending style.

What made the story even more interesting was that he knit the hat himself. While this colourful tidbit made him a household name in Quebec, the toque-wearing ritual did not endear him to the crusty old traditionalist, Dick Irvin.

When Plante was called up to replace McNeil, Irvin already knew about the toque. Irvin felt that there was no bloody way that Plante was going to denigrate the uniform of the Montreal Canadiens by wearing something a child playing on the schoolyard rink would don. This was professional hockey, and in his opinion, a toque on the head of a goalie in the NHL, particularly in the hallowed Forum, was far from professional.

Plante quietly stood his ground — for a while. He even had support from many members of the media, as well as fans who had followed his career. In both the English and French newspapers, Irvin was accused of trying to wreck the young man's confidence by taking away his beloved good-luck charm.

Irvin told Plante that there was an NHL rule prohibiting the wearing of toques, and his view ruled the day. In fact there was no such rule. The young goaltender, not wanting to ruin his chance to play in the NHL, relented.

Plante won two of the three games he played, and tied the other one, all without the toque, allowing only four total goals, for a GAA of 1.33. He told the media that he would never wear a toque again, since he had proved that he could be successful without it.

Jacques Plante was more than just a great goaltender. He had the temperament and carriage of an artist. He was an innovator, a philosopher, an intense student of the game. He was opinionated, fearless, and, in an era when outside interests were frowned upon by the hockey establishment, Plante was a well-rounded Renaissance man.

From a very young age, the game of hockey captivated him. The speed, the grace, the passion for the game infused every fibre of his being and steeled his nerves. As a youngster, he vowed he would become a professional hockey player. And when he did, it would be as an inhabitant of the iron and mesh cage — as a goaltender. Although he would have preferred to play out, he knew that his chronic, and occasionally debilitating, asthma would prevent him from playing any other position.

A single-minded resolve and a confidence that bordered on cockiness were early traits that set Plante apart from his contemporaries while growing up in the hard-working Quebec community of Shawinigan.

As with many French-Canadian families in the very Catholic province, the Plantes were blessed with many children. As the eldest of nine, Jacques was expected to help raise his younger siblings, as well as help out around the house with a variety of chores. As a result, he became adept at a number of home-making skills, including cooking.

When he complained to his mother one day that his ears were getting cold from playing hockey outside, she showed him how to knit, and Plante loved it. Thus, part of the Plante mystique was born. Later, he would knit his own sweaters, hockey socks, and long underwear, and the knitting habit continued for the rest of his life. While in the NHL, when the team travelled by train, most of the players would play cards, but Plante would be off by himself, knitting.

In the 1930s and 1940s, Plante would hang around the outdoor rinks and watch the older kids play hockey. He was a quick study, learning how the passing plays worked, how players positioned themselves for shots, and how goaltenders set themselves for the different plays.

He watched all of this, and realized that he was as good

as the goalies he observed. But he was too young, and thus had little opportunity to test his skills and his mettle. It would take a bit of luck, and a bold move for him to reach the next level.

At about age 12, he was hanging around the outdoor ice rink one day, watching the high school hockey team practice. Out of the blue, a shouting match erupted between the coach and his goalie. The offending teen was banished from the ice.

Suddenly, the coach heard a beckoning voice from the other side of the boards. It was that skinny kid — the one with the intense eyes and angular face, who always silently watched the team go through its paces. Young Jacques Plante offered to fill in for the offending goalie, and before the coach could respond, the impetuous youngster was halfway across the ice, goalie pads in place.

Not only did Plante hold his own against these much older and stronger players, he excelled. The team had a new goalie.

That boldness also served him well when it came to moving up the hockey ladder only a couple of years later. At age 14, he began to hang around the team entrance of the town's only indoor arena. One day, he noticed that the intermediate team, with players ranging in age from 18 to mid-20s, was missing its second goalie. He offered to practice with the team. The coach was impressed with his forthrightness, and decided he had nothing to lose by letting the lean, young man get blistered and battered with a few shots from the big boys.

The coach became the student on this day, as Plante stopped practically everything fired his way. The arena manager stopped what he was doing and came over to the boards to watch the spectacle up close, and later pulled Plante aside and told him that he could hit the ice any time he wanted. Soon, Jacques Plante became a local legend, playing for the midget, juvenile, junior, and intermediate teams — all at the same time.

By his late teens, Plante was in high demand. Junior teams from across Quebec, and even some professional squads from as far away as England and Rhode Island wanted his services.

Plante may have been confident of his abilities as a goalie, but the idea of moving far away from home was too daunting a notion.

While working as a clerk in a local factory after graduating from high school, Plant was offered $85 a week by the Quebec Citadelles junior team, who outbid the Montreal Junior Canadiens' paltry $15.

Plante's independent nature and his inherent intelligence told him that if the Canadiens were interested in him now, they would still be interested in him while he played up the road in Quebec City.

After only two years of junior hockey, including an awesome second season in which the Citadelles beat the Junior

Canadiens for the league title, the young puck-stopper was brought into the Canadiens' fold, signing a contract to play with the minor pro Montreal Royals.

He soon was building his resume as the best young goalie in the minor leagues, and was brought up to the Canadiens for three games in November 1952.

In the playoffs that season, the Canadiens were in tough against the Chicago Blackhawks in the semi-finals. It looked as though the Hawks were going to shunt aside the Habs in six games, as they held a 3-2 advantage in the best-of-seven series. The sixth game was to be played in the raucous Chicago Stadium, the most intimidating building in the league at the time.

The Canadiens had not won a Stanley Cup since 1944, and the fans, media, and team management alike were all putting pressure on coach Irvin to produce a winner. He decided that bold moves were needed. A number of veterans were sat and replaced by lesser-used players, to try and shake up the forward lines, in particular. But the boldest stroke came when McNeil, who had been showing signs of losing his nerve and was not playing well, was yanked in favour of Plante.

Although a star in the Quebec Senior League and now with Buffalo in the AHL, Plante had never faced this kind of pressure before. At the very least, Irvin thought, it would provide a charge throughout the dressing room.

As the story goes, Plante encountered Irvin in the lobby of the team's hotel in Chicago.

"I'll never forget it," Plante told Irvin's son and name-sake, many years later. "I was walking through the hotel lobby in the morning, and your dad called me over. 'You're playing tonight and you're going to get a shutout,' was all he said to me before he walked away."

The final score that night — April 4, 1953 — was 3-0 for Montreal. Plante got his shutout, and also the win the next game, to propel the team into the finals, where they met up with the Boston Bruins.

Plante was inconsistent in that series, winning the first game but losing the second. McNeil then came in and won three straight games, and the Canadiens brought home the Stanley Cup.

McNeil seemed to be back to his old form, and played the bulk of the 1953–1954 season, with Plante getting in only 17 games in the NHL. The rest of the time, he toiled in Buffalo. Then, at the end of the season, McNeil decided to retire, and Plante became the number one goalie for the Montreal Canadiens. With him in goal, the team continued to build and grow stronger, eventually dominating the league.

After the 1954–55 season, Irvin left the team and was replaced by Toe Blake. As the new coach, Blake inherited an incredibly talented team, from the net out.

With Plante ensconced in the net, and the likes of Jean Beliveau, Doug Harvey, Boom Boom Geoffrion, and two Richards — Maurice and later Henri, the Canadiens won the Stanley Cup five consecutive years starting in 1956, and became the most offensively explosive team in NHL history to that point. They helped their netminder, Plante, win the Vezina Trophy those same five years.

Besides becoming one of the all-time greats because of his wonderful talent, ability, and unparalleled success, the innovator in Plante also came to the fore. And, again it was because of what he wanted to wear on his head.

The story of "the mask" probably began in Chicago. On November 11, 1954, just a few weeks into his first full season in Montreal, Plante was taking shots from his teammates in the warm-up before the game. Normally attentive, on this occasion, Plante didn't see the puck coming at him from the stick of Bert Olmstead. It struck him with considerable force on the side of his head. Dropping to the ice in a crumpled, bloody heap, Plante had a fractured cheekbone, and began to consider the notion that standing bare-faced in front of hard rubber projectiles was not a smart idea.

It wasn't until nearly four years later that Plante took action on the notion that had been drifting around in the back of his mind. In a playoff game against Boston in 1958, he took another shot to the noggin and was knocked out.

After the game, Bill Burchmore, who worked for a company called Fiberglass Canada, approached him. He said he had an idea for some facial protection. The two worked together, and with the help of the Canadiens' trainer, developed the prototype of a goalie mask.

After a great deal of urging from Plante, Coach Blake allowed him to wear the mask in practice, but not in a game.

Plante and Blake would argue over the use of a mask for months, often in the media. Blake once said that a goalie who wore a mask was a chicken. Blake, like Irvin, didn't care for revolutionary ideas. He argued that the world was not ready for masked men between the pipes. Not only did a mask convey the message that a goalie was afraid, but it also restricted his vision, the coach asserted. A number of other NHL managers backed him up, including the Rangers' Muzz Patrick, who believed it was a slippery slope. He felt if goalies began wearing masks, it would take away from the fan enjoyment of the game, as they couldn't see their faces. He also felt that position players may want to start wearing helmets and masks, too.

The naysayers prompted a rebuke from NHL president, Clarence Campbell, who was one of the few people of influence in the league who backed Plante.

"It's completely ridiculous for anyone to think a goalie who wants to wear a mask is chicken, because anyone who would stand up to a 100-mile-an-hour projectile is no coward. No goalie has to play without a mask to prove his courage as far as I'm concerned," Campbell told reporters.

On November 1, 1959, the face of hockey changed forever. Plante and the Canadiens were in New York's Madison Square Garden to play the Rangers. Three minutes into the first period, this is how one of the most famous plays in hockey developed, seen through the eyes of Boom Boom Geoffrion.

Jacques Plante

"… Andy Bathgate went down the right side over the blue line. He moved diagonally toward the goal, going from right to left and let a hard backhand shot go. It was probably traveling upwards of 60 miles an hour at a screened goaltender. Jacques never saw it. The puck smacked him right between the nose and mouth. He went down like a redwood that had just been chain sawed. Blood was gushing everywhere."

Bathgate adds, "Earlier in the game Plante went behind the net and gave me a pretty good hip check. The next time I got the puck, I thought I'd get even, so I flipped it at his face.

I didn't even think I hit him, but I did. It wasn't a hard shot. I just flipped it."

Hard or not, the damage had been done. An ugly pool of blood on the white ice at Madison Square Garden testified to that.

After being stitched up by the Rangers' doctor, Plante sent word to Blake that he wouldn't be returning unless he could wear the mask. After initially protesting, Blake relented. When Plante came back onto the ice, he received a rousing ovation from the New York fans, but then drew gasps when he slipped a strange contraption over his head. Cream-coloured, the fibreglass device looked like something from a B-movie.

Before he was hurt, Plante had stopped all three shots he faced. After donning the mask, he stopped 24 of 25 to earn the win. Plante then went undefeated in 10 games, winning nine and tying one, before losing 1-0 to Toronto on December 2. The mask proved to be no impediment to his play.

Later in the season, when his play seemed to slip, he was asked by Blake to at least try playing a game without a mask. On March 8, 1960, he was beaten 3-0 by Detroit. Plante never played without the mask again.

Other goalies began to copy Plante, including his rival in Detroit — Terry Sawchuk. Others held out — Gump Worsley of the Rangers didn't don a mask until the final eight games of his career — in 1974. While Clint Benedict may have been the first NHL netminder to wear facial protection, back in 1930, it took 29 years, and a stubborn, independent netminder from Shawinigan to make it an integral part of a goaltender's gear.

Blake's irritation with Plante continued. Plante always seemed to be coming up with inconvenient health issues. Back then, few people really understood what asthma was and its triggers and effects on sufferers. Many times, Plante would tear at Blake's nerves because at one point during the day he said he wasn't feeling well enough to play, but then would change his mind just before game time.

As the 1950s became the 1960s, the Canadiens were losing their position as the dominant team in the league largely due to the retirement of Rocket Richard after the fifth Cup in 1960. Doug Harvey was dealt to the Rangers at the end of the following season, and Plante's play and personality were perceived as becoming more erratic.

When you're winning and playing at the top of your game, quirks and idiosyncrasies can be ignored. When you're no longer seen as being at your best, they become excuses and distractions.

In the 1960–1961 season, Blake and team management began to question Plante's commitment to the game and to his team. It was Plante's *annus horribilis*. Not even brilliant performances in the semi-finals against Chicago helped him escape the barbs of criticism. Plante knew 1961–1962 would have to be better.

While still wary of the possibility of a return to the bizarre behaviour of the past, both Blake and Selke were confident that their all-star netminder could return to form. They could see it in his eyes, as he arrived at training camp with a renewed intensity, and in the best physical shape of his career.

Plante knew he had a lot to prove. He needed to show that he could still be the best goalie in the world without the stabilizing presence of the brilliant Doug Harvey on the blue line.

"Doug Harvey is the greatest defenceman in the National Hockey League. All of us, especially me, owe him a lot. He helped me win five Vezinas in a row. But I'm going to show you how good Jacques Plante is. I'm going to win the Vezina without him," he declared.

He was certainly a man of his word. While the team didn't win the Stanley Cup, Plante's performance was nothing short of impressive. He played in all 70 games, winning 42, losing 14, and tying 14 more. He had a 2.37 GAA, which garnered him his sixth Vezina Trophy. He was also named the Hart Trophy winner as the NHL's most valuable player.

Only two other goalies, Roy Worters in 1929, and Chuck Rayner in 1950, had won the award. A netminder didn't see his name engraved on that trophy for another 35 years, when Dominik Hasek won it in 1997.

Plante was criticized for his play in the 1962 playoffs, and the downturn seemed to continue into the next season. Never one to shy away from expressing an opinion, or offering his analysis, Plante began yapping to the media during the opening round of the playoffs in 1963. He claimed his team lacked fire and leadership — and he named names. It was no way to endear himself to the rest of the Habs "family."

When Montreal bombed out of the playoffs again, the patience of Canadiens management had reached its limit. Jacques Plante would be wearing a different uniform for the 1962–1963 season.

Plante heard about his trade to New York over the radio. He was being dealt to the Rangers, the perennial doormat of the NHL. Along with Plante went Don Marshall and Phil Goyette. In return came goalie Lorne "Gump" Worsley, Dave Balon, Leon Rochefort, and Len Ronson.

Many in the French-Canadien media castigated Frank Selke, but he and the rest of the Canadiens management team were unrepentant. "Jacques Plante is an extrovert who can't put his personal interests aside for the benefit of the team. In the circumstances, no matter how brilliant a goaltender may be, it was better that he left," Selke told the media.

In New York, Plante was neither happy nor effective. The Rangers hadn't been a serious contender for a number of years. Sore, discouraged, and unimpressed with the coaching of Red Sullivan, Jacques Plante retired shortly after the 1964–1965 season ended, taking an executive sales position with Molson Breweries, the company that owned the Canadiens.

In the fall of that year, Scotty Bowman, the coach of the Montreal Junior Canadiens, asked Plante if he would be interested in tending the nets when they faced off against a touring top Russian team.

When Plante accepted the invitation, it sent a ripple of excitement through the city of Montreal. A packed house of more than 15,000 people showed up at the Forum to see Plante in a Canadiens uniform again. And he didn't disappoint, impressing not only the fans, but Bowman and legendary Soviet hockey guru, Anatoli Tarasov. "I am speechless when I see him play. I hope I can say that the Russian team deserved to meet such a great goaltender. It was a great honour to play against him."

After Bowman moved on to help coach and manage the expansion St. Louis Blues in 1967–1968, he knew that Plante could help his defensive-minded club. In the expansion draft, the Blues had selected Glenn Hall. Bowman wanted veteran insurance in goal, in case Hall got hurt. After Hall lead the Blues to the finals in 1968, Bowman talked Plante into returning to the NHL for the start of the 1968–1969 season. In 37 games, he won 18, lost 12 and tied 6. His 1.96 GAA, combined with Hall's stellar numbers, earned the gray-haired duo the Vezina Trophy. It was Plante's seventh.

After another solid season in 1969–1970, Plante's rights were traded to Toronto. In 40 games for the Maple Leafs in the following season, Plante continued to amaze hockey observers, posting 24 wins and a 1.88 GAA.

Toronto traded Plante to Boston in March 1973. He played only eight games for Boston, before retiring again.

He was lured to be the general manager for the Quebec Nordiques of the World Hockey Association, but that stint lasted only a few weeks. Jacques Plante's illustrious playing career ended with 31 games in the uniform of the Edmonton Oilers of the World Hockey Association (WHA), in the 1974–1975 season.

At age 45, he intended on coming to training camp for Edmonton in the fall of 1975, but he retired for good upon learning of the death of his youngest son. Plante worked with a number of NHL teams as a goalie consultant, before moving to Switzerland in 1979, but would come back to Canada to act as a television hockey analyst. In 1978, he was inducted into the Hockey Hall of Fame with Marcel Pronovost and Andy Bathgate — the man who fired the shot that changed the face of hockey.

Not long after being named to the Montreal Canadiens Dream Team by fans, Plante died of stomach cancer on February 27, 1986.

Chapter 5
Gump Worsley: A Funny Little Hall of Famer

t was the seventh and deciding game of the 1965 Stanley Cup finals, and the Montreal Canadiens were facing the Chicago Blackhawks.

The Habs' number one goalie, Gump Worsley, a veteran of 13 professional hockey seasons, had hurt himself in the previous game, tweaking a knee that had given him trouble off and on throughout his career.

Even though it was the most important game in this season, Habs coach Toe Blake decided to rest Worsley and start a purportedly healthier Charlie Hodge.

Worsley, figuring he could relax, grabbed a booth in the coffee lounge in the Forum, along with his wife, Doreen, and

Blake's wife. Suddenly, a dishevelled and red-faced Montreal trainer, Red Aubut, burst in and made a beeline for Worsley.

Panicked and out of breath, Aubut told Worsley that he had to suit up against Chicago, because Hodge had pulled up lame in the pre-game warm-up.

Ever the wisecracker, Worsley at first thought that the joke might be on him for a change. He was the king of the laconic jab in the Habs dressing room; a lot of players had been the butt of his one-liners and ribbings. Maybe someone was getting even. He shooed Aubut away, but he wouldn't leave. Worsley, who was ready for a splendid evening of watching hockey from the cozy confines of the press box, soon realized that it was no joke.

By the end of the game, it might have seemed a cruel joke to the Hawks, who lost the game 4-0 to the pudgy little goalie with the crew cut hairdo and nerves of steel.

Gump Worsley's greatest asset may be his sense of humour — his ability to look on the lighter side of any situation — even in the stress-filled world of professional hockey netminding. But there was more to Worsley than jokes and japes.

His candid honesty and jocularity had earned him legions of fans and friends within the game, but it was his fearlessness, quick reflexes, and uncanny ability to stick up any number of appendages while flopping around on the ice that got his name enshrined in the Hockey Hall of Fame. Those skills ultimately helped him win four Stanley Cups and earn the Vezina Trophy as the league's top goalie on two occasions.

Not surprisingly, it was his cock-eyed way of looking at life; his relaxed, jolly demeanour; and the permanent twinkle in his eye that allowed him to survive the vagaries of pro hockey until the ancient age of 45. And he was also likely a little crazy. He was pretty sure that most goalies were.

Keeping his feet firmly planted on the ground and not taking life all that seriously probably saved his sanity. Worsley survived the ups and downs of hockey, the disheartening demotions to the minors, venom-spewing coaches who hated his guts (or more accurately, his somewhat paunchy gut), and innumerable injuries to practically every part of his anatomy.

Gump's father, Bill Worsley, was an ironworker who lived with his young family in the cozy but modest Point St. Charles neighbourhood of Montreal. In the midst of these hard-working and hard-living surroundings, Lorne Worsley was born in 1929. When Lorne was a boy, his friends thought he resembled an old-time cartoon strip character named Andy Gump, and the legendary nickname was born.

Worsley's high school hockey coach, Phil Walton, saw the enthusiasm young Lorne had for the game of hockey, but at age 14, Worsley was still less than five feet tall. The young Gumper was told that if he harboured any dreams of playing hockey at a competitive level, he would have to learn to stop pucks. So, a goalie he became.

He carried both his determination to make it as a hockey player and his quirky personality with him when he played for the Montreal suburb of Verdun's junior hockey team — the Cyclones.

He only played two years of major junior hockey in Quebec, but it was against some stiff competition. Jacques Plante, who would go on to his own lengthy and legendary career, played for Quebec City; Bernard Geoffrion, later dubbed "Boom Boom," played for Montreal; and the elegant Jean Beliveau was just beginning to start his storied career, with his hometown Victoriaville Tigres.

The Cyclones were sponsored by the New York Rangers, so all players on their roster were the property of the NHL club from the Big Apple.

While Worsley may have preferred playing for the organization based in his hometown, he was just happy to be playing and getting paid a little bit for it. Each year, he and every other player in the Rangers organization would come to training camp. For two years, Worsley knew he would be sent to the minors.

Then, two parts of the Gump legend resulted from events one evening after a training camp practice before the start of the 1952–1953 NHL season. One was his reputation for enjoying alcohol, and the other was his nasty relationship with Phil Watson.

Watson was a coach in the Rangers minor league system, after 13 years of solid, tough service to the Broadway

Blueshirts throughout the 1930s and 1940s. His reputation as a player with a volcanic temper and prickly personality had not abated when he became a coach.

Watson must not have liked something about Worsley from the start. Perhaps it was his laissez-faire attitude to practice, his jokey personality, or the excess baggage he carried around his mid-section. He had heard that Worsley was a bit of a drinker, and decided to teach the young whipper-snapper a lesson by challenging him to a boozing contest.

Belt after belt disappeared down their throats, as the players crowded round. Suddenly, Watson's visage changed. He turned pale and began to sweat. Then his eyes went glassy as he slumped forward and nearly fell off his chair. Watson had passed out. Worsley let out a satisfied burp, struggled to his feet, and staggered from the room, to the acclaim of his teammates.

Although Watson held a hate-on for some time, he also recognized that the plucky, portly, little netminder was arguably the best and most competitive player on his roster.

Throughout training camp, Worsley knew he was going to continue to be the understudy of veteran Chuck Rayner, but he also knew that Rayner was near the end of his career.

The Rangers liked what they saw of Worsley back when he was playing junior in Verdun. They signed him to a pro contract in 1949, and he was on his way to New York to play with the Rangers EAHL affiliate — the Rovers — getting in a two-game stint with the New Haven Ramblers of the

American Hockey League, the top professional circuit outside of the NHL. Eventually, he was called up to the Rangers to replace an injured Rayner.

The Rangers were a miserable team to behold for most of Worsley's 11-year tenure. Gump won the league's Calder Trophy as its top rookie in 1953. On the surface, his record of 13-29-9, with a GAA of 3.06 hardly seems worthy of a major trophy, but considering the Rangers were perennially at or near the bottom of the league standings, and gave up the most shots on goal, Worsley's efforts were nothing short of heroic. He was a great competitor, who fought to stop pucks game in and game out.

But there was a glimmer of hope on the horizon for the fans who regularly trudged down to Madison Square Garden to see their team. From 1955 to 1960, the Rangers performance was actually respectable under the fire-and-brimstone philosophy of former NHL tough guy Phil Watson.

While he may have been successful on the ice, most of Watson's players reviled his old-school tactics, cutting remarks, and the way he berated and humiliated individual players both in the press and in the dressing room. He may have known about hockey, but he knew little about motivating a man to play his best.

Watson and Worsley loathed each other. Legend has it that once, when they were both guests on a sports-related television in Montreal, they spent much of their time on camera trading barbs. Watson berated Worsley for being fat, for drinking and eating too much, and for not working hard in practice. For his part, Worsley wished Watson would just shut up and let him do his job — which was stopping pucks, not watching his waistline.

Worsley ultimately prevailed in the skirmish. Watson's sandpaper-like personality grated even on the Rangers management, and they finally tired of his antics partway through the 1959–1960 season, when he was fired.

Playing for the New York Rangers for most of the 1950s, and into the 1960s, Worsley arguably had more vulcanized rubber blasted at him than any of his contemporaries in the meshed cage. Often facing as many as 40 shots in a game, and watching his defencemen melt away in front of him, Worsley was bound to get hurt, especially with some of the howitzer-like cannons coming in on him.

One night, former junior hockey nemesis Bernard Geoffrion, who in his autobiography, referred to Worsley as his favourite target, nearly ended Gump's career. Boom Boom came by his nickname honestly. A talented forward with a zest for life and love for the game, the big winger was also blessed with the hardest shot at the time.

In a game played in the mid-1950s, Geoffrion bore down on a virtually unprotected Worsley. The Habs star wound up and unleashed a blast that was rising a little faster than he intended. It was heading straight for the crew-cut-sporting noggin of Gump Worsley.

"Fortunately, I saw it coming and turned my face a bit.

It hit me flat and bounced 25 rows up into the seats. It cut me, but a goalie would rather have a good, clean cut than a bruise. A cut releases the pressure; a bruise just keeps on hurting," he said.

Later in his career, a shot off the stick of Bobby Hull could have put Gump out of the game of hockey and maybe worse. It happened after he had been traded to the Canadiens. In the 1964–1965 season, the Chicago Blackhawks were the team on the rise. They had won the Stanley Cup in 1961, and probably should have won more, thanks to the potent firepower of Bobby and Dennis Hull, and the shifty Stan Mikita.

The Hawks were leading 7-0 in one particularly lop-sided encounter, but were still pressing the attack against Worsley and the rest of the Canadiens. With about 30 seconds left on the clock in the third period, the Golden Jet streaked down the left boards, looking as though he was going to pass. Worsley thought he was too close to the boards to be able to really wind up, and momentarily averted his gaze away from the Golden Jet to see which teammate he might pass to.

Wrong move. That instant of shifted attention was all Hull needed to unleash one of his deadly shots. When Worsley saw the wind-up out of the corner of his eye, it was too late. The puck was already on its way — at more than 100 miles an hour.

"I turned and it hit me in the ear. I dropped, and if there had been a boxing referee there he'd have been counting '110,

111, 112.' They got the smelling salts and propped me up to finish the game," Worsley said many years later.

Worsley said that in the remaining few seconds of the game, no Chicago player fired a shot at him, knowing that he was probably in no position to defend himself. After the game, Hull, one of the true sportsmen of the game, saw Worsley being helped out the arena door with the assistance of a trainer, and came over to check on him.

Luck saved Worsley that night, as the projectile turned on its side and hit Worsley flat on the face. If the thin edge had caught him, we might be talking about the late Gump Worsley.

Players knew that an injury meant the potential loss of a livelihood. In the 1950s and 1960s, players were not raking in multi-million dollar salaries, and often had to supplement their meager NHL income with jobs each summer. There were only six teams in the NHL, so only six starting goaltender jobs were available. If you were out with an injury for any length of time, you risked being replaced — especially if your prospective replacement was younger and cheaper.

Players like Worsley knew they would have to play through pain to keep their jobs. They also didn't want to acknowledge just how risky their jobs really were.

"If you get scared, you're gonna tighten. You're gonna pull up, and then you're through; you've gotta get out," Worsley said. "That's why, in the old days we used to go right back in the net when we got hurt. You can't sit around thinking, 'Hey, I could have lost an eye.'"

Gump Worsley: A Funny Little Hall of Famer

In 1963, Worsley was traded to Montreal for the mercurial Jacques Plante, whose increasingly idiosyncratic personality drove his teammates, and more importantly, his coach Toe Blake, to distraction. When Worsley got injured, Charlie Hodge replaced him. He played down with the AHL's Quebec Aces for the better part of two seasons, before being recalled to start in Montreal towards the end of the 1964–1965 season — just in time for the stretch run, and the race to the Stanley Cup.

Playing in eight post-season games, including the remarkable 4-0 win in the seventh game of the finals, Worsley posted an incredible 1.68 GAA.

Worsley noticed a few things that were different about Montreal compared with his old stomping grounds of New York. The press and fan scrutiny were much more suffocating, but at the same time, the accolades could be far more rewarding. Because the team was only a few years removed from their Rocket-led dynasty of the late 1950s, winning was not an option — it was expected. If you lost two games in a row in New York, hardly anyone noticed. In Montreal, you were a bum.

As well, the cast of characters in front of Worsley was far more talented than the one that suited up in front of him in New York. It included the likes of Jean Beliveau, Henri Richard, Yvan Cournoyer, Ralph Backstrom, and the bruising John Ferguson.

With Worsley in goal, the Canadiens hoisted the Stanley

Cup, somewhat unexpectedly, in 1965, and then again in 1966, defeating Gordie Howe and the Red Wings in six games.

In 1967, the Canadiens were favourites to win again in the finals, expecting to bring the Cup to the Quebec Pavilion at Expo '67. But they underestimated the grit of their opponents, a team of oldtimers from Toronto — particularly veteran netminders Johnny Bower, the man who jockeyed with Worsley for position in New York 14 years earlier, and the inimitable Terry Sawchuk.

The league expanded before the start of the 1967–1968 season, but Montreal was able to hold on to both Worsley and youngster Rogie Vachon, instead of seeing them drafted by an expansion team. The Canadiens were expected to be a decent, if unspectacular team, but thanks to standout goaltending that earned the Worsley–Vachon tandem a Vezina Trophy — the Gumper's second — Montreal went on to win the Stanley Cup that spring.

Partway through the 1968–1969 campaign, it looked as though Worsley was nearing the end of the line. His playing time was decreasing, and he was beginning to develop the first signs of an anxiety disorder.

Always afraid of flying, his anxiety began to increase on road trips in the 1968–1969 season. On a flight to Los Angeles, there was some severe turbulence. When the plane made a stopover, a shaken Worsley scurried back to Montreal, thinking he was done with hockey. The pressure of playing in Montreal, coupled with his fear of flying, had got the best of him,

Worsley was given time to recover by the Canadiens organization, who knew it would not be in the best interests of either Worsley or the hockey club to rush him back.

When he was ready to return, manager Sam Pollock argued that he should go down to the Canadiens farm team to get back into playing shape, promising he would be called up as soon as possible. Worsley said he was ready to play in the NHL now, and would only suit up for the Canadiens. When Pollock insisted on the demotion, Worsley, the 40-year-old veteran, who had seen his fill of minor league bus rides, quit the team.

Worsley, whose decision was backed by wife, Doreen, figured his hockey playing days were over. But Wren Blair, manager of the faltering Minnesota North Stars, came calling. Blair convinced Worsley that if he could get Pollock to trade his rights to him, Gump would like playing in Minnesota.

Worsley joined the North Stars, who were in tough, and not expected to make the playoffs. In his first game with the North Stars, his new team proceeded to lay an 8-0 thumping on the Toronto Maple Leafs. Playing inspired hockey, with a vigour that belied his age, Worsley helped get the North Stars into the playoffs, creating a love affair with the city that lasts to this day.

While he never played more than 34 games with Minnesota that year, sharing the goaltending chores with Cesare Maniago, Worsley compiled some very respectable statistics, astounding fans, teammates, and opponents alike.

Gump Worsley

On February 7, 1971, the North Stars were playing the best team in hockey — the Boston Bruins. The Bruins were deep, talented, tough, and nearly unbeatable. Facing the likes of Bobby Orr, Phil Esposito, Ken Hodge, and Johnny Bucyk — the most awesome offensive force at the time — Worsley displayed an uncanny knack for being in the right place to make the right save at the right time.

Time and again, Orr, the best offensive defenceman in the game, and Esposito, the best power forward in all of hockey, were stymied by the wily old veteran between the pipes. Some of the saves were acrobatic beyond the Gumper's years; others were simply the result of instinctive reactions honed by years of facing shots by the Richard brothers and Boom Boom Geoffrion.

The crowd was on its feet by the end of the game, in appreciation of the effort and the performance of stellar netminding they had just witnessed. The Bruins were not in a mood to applaud. As the final buzzer sounded, some of them looked up at the scoreboard, which showed a 1-1 final, and shook their heads in disbelief. Gump Worsley, with his graying crew cut, ample jowls and rotund belly, had stopped 63 of 64 shots from the most potent offence the game had ever seen up until that point. The old Gumper had taught the cocky Bruins a thing or two.

While the Bruins left the ice with expressions of ill humour, the crowd in Minneapolis roared its approval. The performance made all the newspaper wire services, as well as many end-of-season recaps.

But Worsley refused to be too impressed by his own performance. "The way I played tonight, I must have made the old-timers feel good," he humbly said in the dressing room afterwards.

The old-timers continued to feel pretty good right up until the 1973–1974 season, when, after going 8-14-5, and a 3.11 GAA — his highest since his days in New York — Worsley hung up his skates for good.

Chapter 6

Glenn Hall: The Longevity of Mr. Goalie

I t's very cold on the Canadian prairies in winter. In small communities such as Humboldt, Saskatchewan, the flat, desolate wintry landscape was made less dreary by the scrape of skate blades, the rattle of pucks along the boards, and the squeals of kids, as mothers holler for their wee ones to come inside for supper.

During the Great Depression, which hit the prairies harder than other parts of Canada, most families couldn't afford proper sporting equipment. If a kid was lucky, he or she might have an older sibling with some gear that could be passed down. Most of the time, kids had to make do with what they could cobble together, improvising as best they could.

For most communities, there was also nothing in the way of organized sports for young kids. So they were often left to entertain themselves, as their parents tried their best to keep a roof over their heads.

This was the world that Glenn Hall was born into in the fall of 1931. His dad, Henry, was an engineer for the railroad, but didn't work very often in the Dirty Thirties. Henry had to supplement his meager income wherever he could, while his wife, Agnes, raised the kids and took care of the house.

In those days, kids gathered friends together to make their own pick-up games. For Hall, it was baseball in the spring and summer, and shinny hockey in the fall and winter. From the moment he first donned a pair of skates, the diminutive, but feisty, youngster was an effortless skater and a natural leader. He often helped organize games and played a fine forward position. It wasn't until he played high-school level hockey that he switched to the position that would make him a household name, and a legend.

There were two elementary schools in Humboldt: one Catholic, one not. Enterprising teachers of the senior grades decided each school would have a hockey team that would play against one another through a makeshift season. Once in a while, the best players from each team were thrown together to make a travelling team.

By age 12, Hall was the captain of his school's team. One day, he discovered his netminder was not there, and might not be coming back to the team any time soon. As the captain, he asked the other players if someone would like to fill the position. No takers. So, he strapped on the pads himself.

A quick study of the game, Hall quickly developed a unique style of goaltending. He stayed in a low crouch, bending his legs into an inverted "V." Using his strong legs, superb balance, and lightning reflexes, Hall would spread his "wings" — his arms and feet — to make the save. This, along with his propensity to flit and flop on the ice, earned it the nickname "the butterfly style."

The local juvenile team coach noticed his innate talent and called upon Hall to tend goal for them, even though he was three years younger than many of his new teammates. Then when he was 14 years old, the goalie for the Humboldt Indians Junior A team was kicked off the squad, and friends recommended Hall to the coach. Hall soon became a sensation with the Indians and began to attract the attention of the broader hockey community throughout Saskatchewan.

Surprisingly, at this stage of his career, he didn't appear on the radar screen of many NHL scouts. When a friend of Hall was asked by the Detroit Red Wings organization to pass out flyers for an evaluation camp they were hosting in Saskatoon for any interested prospects, Hall decided it was worth a shot. He figured that the worst thing that could happen was that he would be patted on the head, and told to go back to Humboldt, where he was pretty happy anyway.

When he showed up to participate in a scrimmage, he was given some used equipment, including a glove that was much too big for his hand. As the story goes, a veteran Red Wing player came in on Hall. During a scramble in the crease, Hall lost the cumbersome mitt, and when the player came in for another shot, Hall sprang across the crease and grabbed the hard rubber disc with his bare hand!

Although he was sent back to Humboldt, he was not forgotten. After the training camp, former star defenceman Jack Stewart phoned Red Wings boss Jack Adams with the news that he may have just seen the Wings' goalie of the future.

When Adams heard that Detroit's junior team — the Windsor Spitfires — was seeking goaltending help, he recommended Hall to Spits coach, Jimmy Skinner. The following year, Hall won 31 of 43 games he played for Windsor. He also led the league with six shutouts that 1950–1951 season.

While playing junior hockey, Hall had a novel way of dealing with game-day pressure. He began vomiting before games, and sometimes between periods. It has become as famous a trait for Hall as his butterfly style of playing or his incredible resilience. And it carried through the rest of his playing career. Many thought it was because he was so nervous before the game. Hall says that may have been part of the explanation.

"I was just so excited to go out and play that it made me throw up. I thought of it as a strength," he said.

A few years after coming to the NHL, Hall developed another tool to help him calm down before a game. While playing for the Chicago Blackhawks, he wrestled with team trainer Don "Sockeye" Uren.

Glenn Hall

"Glenn would be Sweet Daddy Siki and I'd be Bulldog Brower, and we'd clear the dressing room and go at it hammer and tongs," said Uren. "Anybody who saw us in there thought we were nuts. It was the only way we discovered to release Glenn's tension. But it sure was rough on me, because I'd often be battered and bruised."

The 1952–1953 NHL season proved to be a real treat for fans of stellar netminding. At some point during the campaign, three of the greatest goaltenders in the history of the sport made their big-league debuts — Jacques Plante filling in for Gerry McNeil in Montreal, Lorne "Gump" Worsley in New York spelling Rangers veteran Chuck Rayner, and a smallish kid from Saskatchewan named Glenn Hall between the pipes for Detroit.

Hall had been making a name for himself in the Western Hockey League with the Edmonton Flyers. He was touted as possibly one of the game's all-time greats.

In Detroit, Terry Sawchuk was another hungry, young western-Canadian netminder. Three years earlier, his brilliant play had hastened the demise of Harry Lumley as the Red Wings goaltender.

A pretty smart cookie, Sawchuk had heard the rumbles about the upstart from Edmonton, who might some day take his job. So he was not surprised when Hall was on his way east at the first sign of trouble.

In a shooting drill just before Christmas in 1952, Alex Delvecchio fired a shot that nailed Sawchuk in the foot, cracking a bone in his instep. Hall dazzled as he filled in. In the six games that he played in relief of Sawchuk, the team won four, tied one, and lost only once. "Sometimes it takes a setback like this injury to Sawchuk, to realize there is talent in reserve," said manager Jack Adams.

Sawchuk returned and played well for the remainder of the regular season, winning his second Vezina Trophy. But his play tailed off again in the semi-finals, and the Red Wings were sent packing by an inferior Boston Bruins team.

Adams, who loved to play mind games with his players, declared that the starting goaltending position for the next season would be a showdown between the incumbent Sawchuk and the upstart Hall.

Hall wasn't into mind games, and was already developing a deep dislike for the tactics and temperament of the man who held his hockey future in the palm of his hand. "There was never any question in my mind that Sawchuk was the number one goalie," Hall said many years later. "He was just too good. Mr. Adams might have been sounding off, but there was nothing to it. He also might have wanted Terry to feel insecure before negotiating his contract."

Sawchuk, by all accounts, was nothing short of incredible during camp. Hall was thanked for his solid effort and sent back to the minors. In the back of both their minds was the ever-present realization that Sawchuk was on a short leash, and the first sign of trouble might see Hall back up with the big club.

The Red Wings would win the Stanley Cup in 1954 and again in 1955, which should have cemented Sawchuk's position. But Hall, who was playing excellent hockey in Edmonton, was seen as a more stable personality than the moody Sawchuk, who by then had developed a drinking problem.

During the 1954–1955 season, when Sawchuk's personal demons began to affect his play, Hall was called up and played in two games. He made enough of an impression that

Adams decided Sawchuk would not be with the Red Wings at the start of next season's training camp. He saw Sawchuk as a declining asset, while Hall was on the upswing. But Sawchuk was also at the peak of his performance, and would fetch the most in the trade market.

On May 28, Sawchuk was dealt to the Bruins, and Hall was the Wings' number one goalie. Hall's first year in Detroit was good enough to garner him the Calder Trophy as the NHL's top rookie for 1955–1956. But the Wings couldn't repeat as Stanley Cup champions, losing to the Montreal Canadiens, who won their first of what would be five consecutive Cups.

Hall won 38 games for Detroit that season, but also got on the bad side of Jack Adams for fraternizing with Ted Lindsay, Adams' former favourite, who was the driving force behind the establishment of a players' association.

Adams sometimes put personal issues above good hockey sense, and the way he handled Lindsay and Hall demonstrated his growing irrationality and paranoia.

Hall was the best young goalie in the league, and was on a team that included a roster chock full of offensive and defensive talent. Gordie Howe, Ted Lindsay, Alex Delvecchio, and Red Kelly, along with Hall, should have been the cornerstones of a dynasty that could challenge the mighty Canadiens throughout the 1950s.

Adams saw Lindsay's attempt to organize the players' association as the height of disloyalty. Hall, like Lindsay, was an independent thinker, and a little outspoken himself. He sympathized with the goals of the players' association, and liked Lindsay as a person. Hall exchanged words with Adams during one of Adams' anti-union rantings. Other than Lindsay, no player had ever stood up to Adams that way.

So, out of spite, Jack Adams traded Hall, a former Calder Trophy winner and NHL All Star, along with Lindsay — the gritty left winger who finished second to teammate Howe in the NHL scoring race — to the lowly Chicago Blackhawks in July 1957.

The Red Wings' loss was definitely Chicago's gain, as Hall became the anchor of an improving Chicago team, and Lindsay injected toughness, leadership, and a winning attitude into a young dressing room.

Before the trade, Hall had played in all 70 games in each of the two previous seasons. His streak would stretch to 502 games in total, a record everyone from Wayne Gretzky to Patrick Roy says will never be broken by a goaltender.

Hall and the Blackhawks were soon contenders. At the end of the 1960–1961 season, the Montreal Canadiens were still seen as the team to beat, but were missing their fiery leader, Maurice Richard, who retired at the end of the previous season. A chink in the Habs' armour had been revealed, and the Blackhawks were ready to exploit it.

The Canadiens were, nevertheless, an excellent team, and proved it by finishing first overall in the league, followed by a vastly improved Toronto squad. Chicago was third, and while they were on the rise, they hadn't yet reached the level of offensive explosiveness they would later in the decade.

Even without Maurice Richard, the Canadiens still had his brother Henri, along with Jean Beliveau, Doug Harvey, Boom Boom Geoffrion, Dickie Moore, plus Jacques Plante in net.

As the underdogs, Hall and the Hawks felt little pressure as they faced off against the Habs in the opening round of the playoffs. The teams split the first two games of the series in Montreal, which was a surprise to the Canadiens and their fans.

The third game, back at the boisterous Chicago Stadium, would be pivotal. If the Canadiens won, their playoff savvy and experience would kick in, and they would likely sweep the rest of the series. If the Blackhawks won, anything could happen.

The Stadium was arguably the most intimidating building to play in for the opposing team, especially a playoff game in which the Hawks were playing well. Knowing their team had a shot to win this series whipped the already raucous crowd into a frenzy before the opening face-off on March 26, 1961.

The teams swapped scoring opportunities in the first period, the tension rising on both benches as each second ticked by. Then, partway through the second period, Chicago's Murray Balfour, a former cast-off of the Canadiens, beat Plante to put his team up 1-0.

Glenn Hall: The Longevity of Mr. Goalie

It was bedlam in the sweltering stadium, but the Canadiens simply redoubled their efforts to put the puck behind Hall. The Blackhawks clamped down, feeding off the brilliant performance they were getting from their man in goal.

Montreal coach, Toe Blake, pulled Plante with 16 seconds left in regulation time and the face-off deep in the Chicago zone. In the face-off circle for Montreal was Henri Richard, one of the best face-off men in the game, as well as a potentially explosive offensive threat. He won the draw, and before anyone in the building knew it, he had scored on a surprised Glenn Hall. The game would be decided in overtime.

Hall was angry at himself for letting in a goal at such a critical juncture in the game. They could have been celebrating with a beer or two by now if the Pocket Rocket hadn't scored.

In the second overtime period, it looked as though insult would be heaped atop injury for Hall, as Montreal's Don Marshall batted the puck past him. But the referee ruled Marshall's stick was too high, and the goal was disallowed.

The roller-coaster ride continued as the Canadiens kept pressing, and Hall kept beating them back. Finally, Balfour scored 11 minutes into the third overtime to give Chicago the win. Chicago lost the next game 5-2, but came back to shock the Habs, by winning games five and six by identical scores of 3-0. Hall was the player of the series for Chicago, and their elimination of Montreal meant there was going to be a new Stanley Cup champion for the first time in six years.

Defeating the Red Wings in six games was a fitting denouement to a thrilling season for Hall and the Blackhawks. Chicago had won its first Stanley Cup since 1938.

Hall and teammates Bobby Hull, Pierre Pilote, and Stan Mikita were touted to do big things. Chicago was a young team, a talented team. It was well coached, had incredible fans, and by rights, should have been the dominant team of the 1960s. Instead, the rejuvenated Maple Leafs came to the fore. They weren't flashy, they weren't blessed with an over-abundance of show-stopping talent, but they played solid, workmanlike, often flawless hockey.

They, not the Chicago Blackhawks, won the Stanley Cup in 1962, then again in 1963 and 1964. Disappointment at not being able to convert great regular season performances into Stanley Cups was beginning to wear on fans and Hawks management. But there were still things to cheer about. Hall's consecutive games streak was generating the most attention throughout the 1961–1962 season, and into the following campaign.

Hall's remarkable streak of consecutive games ended on November 2, 1962, when Hall, with very little fanfare, sat out a game due to a nagging leg injury. In typically modest fashion, he summed up the end of the streak:

"Remember, goaltenders were expected to play in almost all the games back then and I have never thought the streak was all that remarkable. I say individual records should always take a back seat to a team accomplishment such as winning the Stanley Cup," he said.

When Toronto wasn't winning Stanley Cups in the mid-1960s, Montreal was. They took the title from the Leafs in 1965, and repeated as champions in 1966. Chicago was always playing the role of the bridesmaid. Since then, Chicago has yet to raise the Stanley Cup. Theirs is currently the longest Stanley Cup drought in the NHL — 45 years by the 2005–2006 season.

Before the 1967–1968 season, the NHL expanded from six to 12 teams. The six existing franchises were allowed to protect two goalies in the system. The Hawks wanted to keep their two young netminders, Denis Dejordy and Dave Dryden, meaning the old guy (with the fatter contract) could be exposed in the expansion draft.

Once Hall deduced that he was not in the Hawks' future plans, he decided to retire. But many hockey insiders felt that Hall could be lured back, if the price was right.

Scotty Bowman was one of those people, as was his new boss with the St. Louis Blues, Lynn Patrick. It was a risky proposition, but the Blues decided to use the second overall pick in the expansion draft to select Hall.

Hall let it be known to all who would listen that St. Louis had wasted their pick. The entire brain trust of the Blues traveled to Stony Plain to visit Hall. After dickering over a contract, they got Hall to sign, with the proviso that he could miss most of training camp. (Hall always hated training camp.)

In his first season with the Blues, he helped give the team instant respectability. In 49 games, Hall won 19, lost 21, and tied another 9. But his GAA was a slender 2.48, second in the entire NHL. The Blues were the best team in the new Western Division. (All six of the expansion teams played in the West. The winner of that division in the playoffs would face the winner of the East, made up of the Original Six clubs.)

But it was in the playoffs that Hall earned his keep. Through the first 12 games, Hall was phenomenal, helping the Blues make it to the finals, where they faced off against the Canadiens. The Blues were swept aside in four straight games, but they were all close. Hall's performance was considered so outstanding that he was awarded the Conn Smythe Trophy as the most valuable player in the playoffs.

The following season, Hall was joined in the St. Louis goaltending stable by another legend, Jacques Plante. Lured out of retirement by Bowman, Plante showed little rust in his three-year layoff. Hall and Plante shared the Vezina Trophy at the end of the 1968–1969 campaign. Montreal again swept the Blues in the finals, but St. Louis had gained the respect of the more established teams in the league. A third straight appearance in the finals saw the Blues go up against the Boston Bruins.

Boston was now the class of the NHL, and featured the most potent offence yet seen in the league, with the likes of Derek Sanderson and Phil Esposito up front. But it was at the defensive end of the ice where the real story of the Bruins' success lay. Bobby Orr had become the single most dominant player in the league that season, leading the entire league in scoring with 33 goals and 87 assists for 120 points, 21 better than teammate Esposito.

The Bruins dominated the first three games of the series, with none of the scores particularly flattering for the Blues. But they played the fourth and ultimately final game of the series much tighter, forcing the Bruins to go into overtime. Hall then played a part in one of the most famous goals in the history of the NHL — Bobby Orr's Stanley Cup–winning goal, scored as he flew through the air after being tripped by Blues defender Noel Picard. It is one of the most famous images in sports history, and poor Hall is the goaltender who suffers the ignominy of being in the frame every time the photo of the goal is reproduced. He retired soon thereafter.

Hall became a goaltending consultant and coach for a number of years, including an extended tenure with the Calgary Flames.

Mike Vernon, now retired from the NHL after winning Stanley Cups with the Flames and Detroit, said he credits Hall for making him a first-rate NHL goaltender.

"Probably one of the best guys I've ever met. He loves the game. He helped me out tremendously. There's more to goaltending than just stopping the puck. There's the mental part, and Glenn is great at settling you down and giving you confidence," said Vernon.

For nearly 20 NHL seasons Glenn Hall gave confidence to every teammate he played with, every coach he worked under, and every fan who ever saw him tend goal.

Chapter 7
Johnny Bower:
Middle-aged Marvel

Hunched over, his powerful legs moving his body from side to side with seemingly effortless ease, his heavy cumbersome pads feeling light as a feather, Johnny Bower perched on the edge of the goalmouth, his eyes fixed on the blade of the stick with the puck on it. In the millisecond before it's released, he tries to anticipate where it's going to go: top shelf? five-hole? stick side along the ice?

It was a familiar sight for Bower fans — his reflexes belied those of a man approaching middle age, as he was peppered with shot after shot, rock-hard rubber projectiles flew at the veteran netminder from all angles. An arm would dart out here, a leg there. If an onrushing puck carrier got a little too close, Bower's huge wooden Northland stick would be flung out at lightning speed, pushing the puck out of harm's way and often knocking the forward onto his backside.

The sweat cascaded in rivulets down the craggy lines on Bower's battle-scarred, but still cherubic, face. Welts marked where a deflected puck or an errant stick had landed against unprotected flesh.

But there was often the flash of a smile underneath the intense piercing gaze. It wasn't the smile of someone who just pulled a fast one on a teammate, or someone proud of his own performance. It was the smile of a middle-aged boy who loved every minute of his life, a man who truly appreciated the gift he had been given — the chance to play in the NHL.

And this was only how Johnny Bower practiced, especially during his tenure with the Toronto Maple Leafs, where he performed brilliantly and became a beloved icon from 1958 to 1970.

In games, he was the picture of intensity, carrying with him onto the frozen playing surface a desperate desire to keep all pucks from getting past him. In practice, that desperation continued, as the aging netminder wouldn't allow his skills to slip even an iota, because that might mean demotion to the minors.

After playing in the minors as long as Bower did, once he got his break, he made the most of it. His incredible longevity (he played until he was 47) and his talent were due to good old-fashioned toil and sweat.

Growing up in rural Saskatchewan, Bower, born in

Johnny Bower: Middle-aged Marvel

Prince Albert in 1924, always seemed to be in goal when he and his chums played hockey. He didn't even seem to care that he had no pads to protect himself for the first few years. When someone donated an old pair to the talented youngster, in the deepest, darkest days of the Great Depression, he treasured them.

Bower, like many other hockey-playing boys in Canada's prairie heartland, learned the game on frozen ponds and sloughs that broke up the flat-as-a-pancake landscape.

As he was beginning to make a name for himself in and around Prince Albert, World War II broke out. Bower didn't want to be caught idle, while young men all around him were going overseas to fight for king and country. In 1940, at age 16, he fibbed about his age and gave a false name — John Kizskan. Actually, it was his birth name, but it was changed to Bower when his dad John discovered people had trouble pronouncing it.

The next thing he knew, he was in the army. Two of his four years in the military were spent overseas. Amazingly, he was still junior-aged when he returned unscathed from the war to restart his hockey career. While with the Prince Albert Black Hawks of the Saskatchewan Junior Hockey League, he had the lowest GAA in the league and attracted the attention of pro scouts.

In 1945–1946, he signed on with the Cleveland Barons of the American Hockey League, a team that didn't have an official affiliation agreement with an NHL club. Bower's start in pro hockey was unimpressive. In his first season, he won 18, lost 17, and boasted an inflated GAA of 3.90. The following year, he had twice as many wins (22) as losses (11) and had begun turning the league on its ear with a unique addition to the goaltending arsenal.

Bower discovered as a young goalie that if he waited until the last moment, and then slid his goal stick out as fast and as far as he could, catching a nub of black hockey tape at the end of the shaft, he could "poke" the puck off the stick of an opposing player. Johnny Bower had invented the poke-check, and used it to great effect in his burgeoning hockey career.

By 1958, Bower was a multi-time all-star in the AHL. He had experienced the thrill of NHL hockey briefly with the New York Rangers a few years earlier. At the same time, Punch Imlach had been brought in to save a moribund Toronto Maple Leafs franchise, and he knew that a team, even a rebuilding one, was only as good as its goaltending.

Punch Imlach's predecessor in the manager's chair at Maple Leaf Gardens, Billy Reay, was actually the man credited with signing Bower away from Cleveland, but it was Imlach who made sure Bower did the things that would keep him in the NHL.

"Old guys like myself and Allan Stanley and Tim Horton liked Punch because we understood the importance of working hard in practice and in the games. I liked Punch. He was tough, but I think that's what's needed to be a winner," said

Bower in a 1999 interview. "He gave me a chance to come back to the NHL. He always told me, though, that if I didn't work hard and didn't perform, I was out."

Since Bower had endured the deprivations of 11 seasons in minor professional hockey, he did not take an NHL career for granted. For Johnny Bower, that work ethic was motivated partly by a sense of foreboding, a concern that the rug could be pulled out from under him at any time. Fear of demotion and fear of injury propelled Bower into his Herculean work patterns in practice.

The monetary rewards were not much greater in the NHL than the AHL. Many hockey players of the Original Six era made what by today's NHL standards would be considered a pathetic pittance. Iron-fisted — and tight-fisted — managers, such as Imlach and Detroit's Jack Adams, could ruin the career of a player who was too demanding, by sending him to the minors and keeping him there. Bower had been there and didn't want to go back, once he got used to life in the NHL.

One example of how the fear and intimidation kept many a player's professional and financial ambitions in check took place in 1964. Early that season, but only after some prompting from team captain George Armstrong, Bower screwed up the courage to ask Imlach for a raise. Armstrong told Bower that he deserved more than the $13,000 he was getting, especially after being a key cog in the Maple Leafs machine that won the Stanley Cup the three previous seasons.

Nervously, Bower asked Imlach for a $10,000 raise one day after practice. Without uttering a word, Imlach ushered him out the door. He was subsequently thrown out of Imlach's office four more times during these contract "negotiations," and eventually netted a raise of $2,500, which Armstrong labelled disgraceful.

"While I was in there, I got thinking of all those years I spent riding those buses in the American League, and how Punch might send me back if I got him mad enough. I never want to ride those buses again," Bower said of the incident.

Bower was not just a hard worker — he was tough. Very tough. You had to be just to make it as a player in the era of Original Six NHL hockey. A goalie had to be even tougher.

His ability to handle pain made Leaf coach Punch Imlach into his number one fan. In later reminiscences, Imlach liked to talk about an incident that happened to Bower in a game played in Detroit against the Red Wings, on February 12, 1961.

Toronto was battling Montreal for first place in the league standings, and Bower had a chance to strip the mantle as the best goaltender in the National Hockey League from perennial Vezina Trophy–winner Jacques Plante of the Canadiens.

Bower went into the corner to try and corral a loose puck, when Howie Young, a man not known for his subtleties or for having any regard for his opponents, slammed into him. Bower lost a tooth, and suffered a serious leg injury close to his hip joint. The hip/leg joint is crucial to a goalie's lateral mobility, which in turn is critical to his ability to stop pucks.

After the hit, Bower could barely stand up, and the agony that was evident on his face was not lost on Imlach. Punch Imlach never believed a little pain should get in the way of a player's performance or a team's success, but even he could see the torment Bower must be enduring. He urged Bower to come over to the bench, which he did, barely. There, Imlach was concerned enough to asked Bower if he wanted to come out.

Bower shook his head and hobbled back to his crease, trying to skate off the pain as best he could.

"I'll never forget the sight of him out there playing the last 12 minutes of the game," Imlach reported. "When he was standing in the goal, he had to hold onto the crossbar with his left hand, to take the weight off his leg. But he kept them out. Talk about guts. Nobody ever, anywhere in sports, had more guts than Bower."

Toronto won the game 4-2, then lost Bower for five weeks due to the serious injury. His deletion from the lineup cost the Maple Leafs first place in the league standings and the opening round of the 1961 playoffs. Without Bower's ability on the ice and his infectious work ethic off it, the Leafs fell to the offensively gifted Chicago Blackhawks.

Over the years, Bower played with broken bones, gaping cuts, welts, and ugly bruises. He was also knocked out on more than one occasion. While with Cleveland in the early 1950s, Bower had nine of his teeth knocked out in a game. The team's trainer — a position that involved little medical training — sewed the wound up with the aid of a flashlight and no anesthetic. Bower's mouth was then frozen (oddly enough, they decided to freeze it after they did the procedure), and he finished the game. But the sutures were brutal and Bower nearly bled to death overnight. After his wife rushed him to two hospitals, Bower endured having the wound reopened and repaired, this time properly, and with anesthetic before the procedure.

He gained admirers throughout the league for his talent, positive attitude, and ability to tolerate pain. By the mid-1960s, Bower was approaching middle age. Imlach decided that Bower could no longer play the entire season like the goalie could when in his 30s. So, in the 1965 off-season, he picked up temperamental veteran Terry Sawchuk and instituted the first real platoon goaltending system.

The experiment didn't translate into immediate Stanley Cup success, as the team saw the rival Canadiens take the chalice in both 1965 and 1966.

When the 1966–1967 season rolled around, the Maple Leafs had cobbled together the oldest lineup in the NHL. Instead of picking up energetic young bucks who could be the mainstays on the roster for years to come, Imlach dealt them away for experience and grit.

He no doubt saw this season as a last gasp for the old

guard, before the NHL expanded from six to 12 teams the following year. Still, critics charged that the Maple Leafs were too decrepit to even make it into the playoffs, let alone win the Stanley Cup that spring. But, led by the ancient goaltending tandem of Bower and Sawchuk, the Over-the-Hill Gang defied the odds and the critics by first making it to the finals, then winning the Cup in six games.

Bower was dressed for the sixth and deciding game at Maple Leaf Gardens, even though he was in no condition to play. It was a sign of the esteem in which he was held by Imlach, who wanted his stalwart netminder to enjoy the fruits of his labour — a possible Stanley Cup win on home ice and in uniform.

Teammate Larry Hillman takes the blame for knocking Bower out of the 1967 finals against the Canadiens. The team was in Montreal, getting ready for game four. Bower was between the pipes, as his teammates streamed in on him, one after the other, firing pucks up, down, and all around.

He had been playing pretty well, but he knew he had to, because his stable-mate, Terry Sawchuk, was pretty banged up. Bower was trying to stop as many shots as he could, when Hillman moved in, along with a couple of other teammates. More than one puck was shot, and Bower tried to stop all of them.

"I was just practicing keeping my shot on the ice, but I shot on his stick side, and since he doesn't like to have anything go in on him — he was that type of guy — he shot his leg over real quick with his stick, and he pulled his groin," said Hillman more than 30 years later. "And that's how he ended up coming out. And Imlach said, 'Who the hell hit Bower?' Well, nobody hit him, he pulled his groin just going to make a stop."

Bower's perfectionism nearly cost the Maple Leafs dearly. With Bower on the shelf, and the series tied at two games apiece, a shaky, injured Sawchuk would now have to carry the Over-the-Hill Gang through the onslaught of Beliveau, the Pocket Rocket, and a young Yvan Cournoyer, if they wanted to win the last Stanley Cup of the Original Six era.

Fortunately, Sawchuk was at his legendary best, and the Toronto Maple Leafs — the aging hockey team with the oldest netminding pair ever — won the Stanley Cup.

Bower was protected when the Maple Leafs drew up their lists for the expansion draft to happen in the summer of 1967. Sawchuk was not. As the dismantling of the great Maple Leaf dynasty of the 1960s began in earnest, he was picked up by Los Angeles. Many other Leafs also went in the expansion draft, while others retired. The youth that should have been so full of promise for the Maple Leafs was nowhere to be seen, as many of the best and brightest young prospects nurtured in the bosom of the Maple Leafs organization were dealt away for secure veteran help.

Bower would be surrounded by a combination of aging veterans, mediocre journeymen, and raw, unproven kids for his remaining tenure as a Maple Leaf.

He played 43 games effectively in 1967–1968, while injuries allowed him to participate in only 20 games the following season. After allowing five goals in the first game he played in the 1969–1970 season, Bower decided that, at age 47, enough was enough.

Still one of the most beloved of former Maple Leafs, Johnny Bower keeps busy with a hockey school that bears his name, and is always in demand for autograph signings and public appearances. Fans, both young and old, continue to line up to shake his hand and bask in that broad, craggy smile.

Acknowledgments

Many books and articles were consulted in researching this book. Quotes were drawn from a number of them including William Brown's *The Montreal Maroons: The Forgotten Stanley Cup Champions* and *The Doug Harvey Story; Gordie: A Hockey Legend,* by Roy MacSkimming; a number of books by Brian McFarlane including nearly all of his Original Six series, as well as his work *Clancy: The King's Story.* Some quotes were also gleaned from the work of Dick Irvin, including his books, *My 26 Stanley Cups: Memories of a Hockey Life, In the Crease: Goaltenders Look at Life in the NHL,* and *Now Back to You Dick: Two Lifetimes in Hockey.* I used some from Boom Boom Geoffrion's autobiography; Andrew Podnieks's *The Goal;* numerous books by the pre-eminent American hockey historian, Stan Fischler, including his *Hockey Stars of 1972* and *Hockey Stars of 1973;* and *After the Applause* and *Breakaway* by Charles Wilkins.

Fortunately, some great biographies have been penned about some of my subjects. David Dupuis authored *Sawchuk: The Troubles and Triumphs of the World's Greatest Goalie,* while Brian Kendall wrote *Shutout: The Legend of Terry Sawchuk.* A quote or two came from them, as did quotes from Raymond Plante's biography of Jacques Plante, and *Glenn Hall: The Man They Call Mr. Goalie* by Ted Adrahtas.

Acknowledgments

I was also able to draw upon many past interviews I have conducted over my years in the newspaper business.

I also thank Kara, Stephen, Ellen, and Jill from Altitude for trusting me with another book, and for their support and encouragement. My pal Chris Gough from the Collingwood Public Library, and Doug Measures from Rogers Television have immensely helped in promoting my previous books.

My wife Sheri, again, put up with a lot of keyboard tapping, page-turning, sighs of frustration, and the odd late night, as her obsessive–compulsive hubby went back into ragged writer mode. She can't be thanked enough.

Photo Credits

Cover: AP Photo; Graphic Artists/Hockey Hall of Fame: page 51; Hockey Hall of Fame: page 36; Imperial Oil–Turofsky/Hockey Hall of Fame: page 67; London Life-Portnoy/Hocky Hall of Fame: pages 86, 93.

Further Reading

Adrahtas, Tom. *Glenn Hall: The Man They Call Mr. Goalie.* Vancouver: Greystone Books, 2002.

Dupuis, David. *Sawchuk: The Troubles and Triumphs of the World's Greatest Goalie.* Toronto: Stoddart Publishing, 1998.

Hunter, Douglas. *Champions: The Illustrated History of Hockey's Greatest Dynasties.* Toronto: Penguin Studio, 1997.

Irvin, Dick. *In the Crease: Goaltenders Look at Life in the NHL.* Toronto: McClelland and Stewart, 1995.

McFarlane, Brian. *Brian McFarlane's Original Six: The Habs.* Toronto: Stoddart Publishing, 1996.

McFarlane, Brian. *Brian McFarlane's Original Six: The Rangers.* 1997.

About the Author

A veteran of more than a dozen years in the community newspaper industry, Jim Barber has won a number of Ontario Community Newspaper Association Awards, as well as a Canadian Community Newspaper Association Award for an editorial he penned about honouring Canadian Korean War veterans. In 2005, he won an award from the Suburban Newspaper Association of America for a story on the 40th anniversary of the death of hockey legend Tim Horton.

Besides writing for the *Amazing Stories* hockey series, Jim works as the Sports, Arts and Lifestyles editor for *The Barrie Advance*. His career has taken him to newspaper assignments in his hometown of Newmarket, as well as Port Colborne, Kirkland Lake, Peterborough, Oshawa, and Collingwood.

Barber has written a book about local hockey stars from the Collingwood area, as well as *Toronto Maple Leafs: Stories of Canada's Legendary Team*, and *Montreal Canadiens: Thrilling Stories from Canada's Famous Hockey Franchise*, for the Amazing Stories imprint.

Educated at Peterborough's Trent University and Centennial College in Toronto, he lives in the village of Nottawa, a few miles from Georgian Bay, with his wife, Sheri, and two teenaged stepsons.

OTHER AMAZING STORIES

These titles are available wherever you buy books. If you have trouble finding the book you want, call the Altitude order desk at **1-800-957-6888**, e-mail your request to: **orderdesk@altitudepublishing.com** or visit our Web site **at www.amazingstories.ca**

New **AMAZING STORIES** titles are published every month.